# THE
# DUTCH
# AMERICANS

# THE DUTCH AMERICANS

Victoria Olsen

**CHELSEA HOUSE PUBLISHERS**
New York   Philadelphia

On the cover: A Dutch American family poses for a photograph in Pella, Iowa, circa 1880.

**CHELSEA HOUSE PUBLISHERS**
Editor-in-Chief: Nancy Toff
Executive Editor: Remmel T. Nunn
Managing Editor: Karyn Gullen Browne
Copy Chief: Juliann Barbato
Picture Editor: Adrian G. Allen
Art Director: Maria Epes
Manufacturing Manager: Gerald Levine

**The Peoples of North America**
Senior Editor: Sean Dolan

**Staff for THE DUTCH AMERICANS**
Associate Editor: Abigail Meisel
Copy Editor: Karen Hammonds
Deputy Copy Chief: Ellen Scordato
Editorial Assistant: Elizabeth Nix
Picture Research: PAR/NYC
Assistant Art Director: Laurie Jewell
Senior Designer: Noreen M. Lamb
Layout: Louise Lippin
Production Coordinator: Joseph Romano
Cover Illustration: Paul Biniasz
Banner Design: Hrana L. Janto

First Printing

1  3  5  7  9  8  6  4  2

**Library of Congress Cataloging-in-Publication Data**
Olsen, Victoria.
    The Dutch Americans.

    (The Peoples of North America)
    Bibliography: p.
    Includes index.
    1. Dutch Americans—Juvenile literature.
I. Title.    II. Series.
E184.D9047  1988        973'.043931        87-33753
ISBN 0-87754-873-0
        0-7910-0288-8 (pbk.)

# CONTENTS

# THE PEOPLES OF NORTH AMERICA

CHELSEA HOUSE PUBLISHERS

# A NATION OF NATIONS

Daniel Patrick Moynihan

The Constitution of the United States begins: "We the People of the United States . . ." Yet, as we know, the United States is not made up of a single group of people. It is made up of many peoples. Immigrants from Europe, Asia, Africa, and Central and South America settled in North America seeking a new life filled with opportunities unavailable in their homeland. Coming from many nations, they forged one nation and made it their own. More than 100 years ago, Walt Whitman expressed this perception of America as a melting pot: "Here is not merely a nation, but a teeming Nation of nations."

Although the ingenuity and acts of courage of these immigrants, our ancestors, shaped the North American way of life, we sometimes take their contributions for granted. This fine series, *The Peoples of North America*, examines the experiences and contributions of the immigrants and how these contributions determined the future of the United States and Canada.

Immigrants did not abandon their ethnic traditions when they reached the shores of North America. Each ethnic group had its own customs and traditions, and each brought different experiences, accomplishments, skills, values, styles of dress, and tastes in food that lingered long after its arrival. Yet this profusion of differences created a singularity, or bond, among the immigrants.

The United States and Canada are unusual in this respect. Whereas religious and ethnic differences have sparked intolerance throughout the rest of the world—from the 17th-century religious wars to the 19th-century nationalist movements in Europe to the near extermination of the Jewish people under Nazi Germany—North Americans have struggled to learn how to respect each other's differences and live in harmony.

Millions of immigrants from scores of homelands brought diversity to our continent. In a mass migration, some 12 million immigrants passed through the waiting rooms of New York's Ellis Island; thousands more came to the West Coast. At first, these immigrants were welcomed because labor was needed to meet the demands of the Industrial Age. Soon, however, the new immigrants faced the prejudice of earlier immigrants who saw them as a burden on the economy. Legislation was passed to limit immigration. The Chinese Exclusion Act of 1882 was among the first laws closing the doors to the promise of America. The Japanese were also effectively excluded by this law. In 1924, Congress set immigration quotas on a country-by-country basis.

Such prejudices might have triggered war, as they did in Europe, but North Americans chose negotiation and compromise, instead. This determination to resolve differences peacefully has been the hallmark of the peoples of North America.

The remarkable ability of Americans to live together as one people was seriously threatened by the issue of slavery. It was a symptom of growing intolerance in the world. Thousands of settlers from the British Isles had arrived in the colonies as indentured servants, agreeing to work for a specified number of years on farms or as apprentices in return for passage to America and room and board. When the first Africans arrived in the then-British colonies during the 17th century, some colonists thought that they too should be treated as indentured servants. Eventually, the question of whether the Africans should be viewed as indentured, like the English, or as slaves who could be owned for life, was considered in a Maryland court. The court's calamitous decree held that blacks were slaves bound to lifelong servitude, and so were their children.

America went through a time of moral examination and civil war before it finally freed African slaves and their descendants. The principle that all people are created equal had faced its greatest challenge and survived.

Yet the court ruling that set blacks apart from other races fanned flames of discrimination that burned long after slavery was abolished—and that still flicker today. The concept of racism had existed for centuries in countries throughout the world. For instance, when the Manchus conquered China in the 17th century, they decreed that Chinese and Manchus could not intermarry. To impress their superiority on the conquered Chinese, the Manchus ordered all Chinese men to wear their hair in a long braid called a queue.

By the 19th century, some intellectuals took up the banner of racism, citing Charles Darwin. Darwin's scientific studies hypothesized that highly evolved animals were dominant over other animals. Some advocates of this theory applied it to humans, asserting that certain races were more highly evolved than others and thus were superior.

This philosophy served as the basis for a new form of discrimination, not only against nonwhite people but also against various ethnic groups. Asians faced harsh discrimination and were depicted by popular 19th-century newspaper cartoonists as depraved, degenerate, and deficient in intelligence. When the Irish flooded American cities to escape the famine in Ireland, the cartoonists caricatured the typical "Paddy" (a common term for Irish immigrants) as an apelike creature with jutting jaw and sloping forehead.

By the 20th century, racism and ethnic prejudice had given rise to virulent theories of a Northern European master race. When Adolf Hitler came to power in Germany in 1933, he popularized the notion of Aryan supremacy. "Aryan," a term referring to the Indo-European races, was applied to so-called superior physical characteristics such as blond hair, blue eyes, and delicate facial features. Anyone with darker and heavier features was considered inferior. Buttressed by these theories, the German Nazi state from

1933 to 1945 set out to destroy European Jews, along with Poles, Russians, and other groups considered inferior. It nearly succeeded. Millions of these people were exterminated.

The tragedies brought on by ethnic and racial intolerance throughout the world demonstrate the importance of North America's efforts to create a society free of prejudice and inequality.

A relatively recent example of the New World's desire to resolve ethnic friction nonviolently is the solution the Canadians found to a conflict between two ethnic groups. A long-standing dispute as to whether Canadian culture was properly English or French resurfaced in the mid-1960s, dividing the peoples of the French-speaking Quebec Province from those of the English-speaking provinces. Relations grew tense, then bitter, then violent. The Royal Commission on Bilingualism and Biculturalism was established to study the growing crisis and to propose measures to ease the tensions. As a result of the commission's recommendations, all official documents and statements from the national government's capital at Ottawa are now issued in both French and English, and bilingual education is encouraged.

The year 1980 marked a coming of age for the United States's ethnic heritage. For the first time, the U.S. Census asked people about their ethnic background. Americans chose from more than 100 groups, including French Basque, Spanish Basque, French Canadian, Afro-American, Peruvian, Armenian, Chinese, and Japanese. The ethnic group with the largest response was English (49.6 million). More than 100 million Americans claimed ancestors from the British Isles, which includes England, Ireland, Wales, and Scotland. There were almost as many Germans (49.2 million) as English. The Irish-American population (40.2 million) was third, but the next largest ethnic group, the Afro-Americans, was a distant fourth (21 million). There was a sizable group of French ancestry (13 million), as well as of Italian (12 million). Poles, Dutch, Swedes, Norwegians, and Russians followed. These groups, and other smaller ones, represent the wondrous profusion of ethnic influences in North America.

Canada, too, has learned more about the diversity of its population. Studies conducted during the French/English conflict showed that Canadians were descended from Ukrainians, Germans, Italians, Chinese, Japanese, native Indians, and Eskimos, among others. Canada found it had no ethnic majority, although nearly half of its immigrant population had come from the British Isles. Canada, like the United States, is a land of immigrants for whom mutual tolerance is a matter of reason as well as principle.

The people of North America are the descendants of one of the greatest migrations in history. And that migration is not over. Koreans, Vietnamese, Nicaraguans, Cubans, and many others are heading for the shores of North America in large numbers. This mix of cultures shapes every aspect of our lives. To understand ourselves, we must know something about our diverse ethnic ancestry. Nothing so defines the North American nations as the motto on the Great Seal of the United States: *E Pluribus Unum*—Out of Many, One. ✎

*A Dutch-American farmer in Michigan cuts grain in about 1900.*

# THE DUTCH THROUGH AMERICAN HISTORY

Since their arrival in the New World in 1624, the Dutch have traveled the path of American history. During the 17th century Dutch fur traders and merchants established a colony—New Netherland—on the east coast of the country. Though this colony remained in Dutch control for only 40 years, its legacy survives in the many Dutch place-names in New York State; such as the New York City boroughs of Brooklyn and the Bronx and the town of Rensselaer in upstate New York.

In the 19th century a second wave of 250,000 Dutch immigrants—many of them refugees from religious persecution—journeyed to America to freely practice their creed. Some remained on the East Coast, near the old communities established by their predecessors in America, but most set out westward. In the mid-1800s they turned wilderness to farmland throughout the Midwest, establishing such towns as Pella, Iowa; Holland, Michigan; and Little Chute, Wisconsin.

Many Dutch who arrived during the 1860s and later pioneered in the frontier territories of the West turned marshland to settlement on land that became the city of Chicago. The migration of Dutch to the United States leveled off after about 1865—the Civil War era—

and remained nominal until the end of World War II. During the postwar years the latest surge of immigrants from the Netherlands, numbering about 80,000, left their war-torn homeland to begin life anew in the nation their ancestors had helped found.

The Dutch traveled to America in much the same way as other immigrants. Until the middle of the 19th century, they left Holland in sailing ships that spent several months crossing the Atlantic Ocean. Passengers lived below the deck in a space that was often only five feet in height and rarely had any portholes to admit light. The boats were grossly overcrowded: Two or three people slept in every bed. These conditions encouraged the spread of disease and, combined with frequent shortages of food and drinking water, caused many deaths. Historians Leonard Dinnerstein and David M. Reimers cited an extreme case in their book *Ethnic Americans*: In 1752 only 21 out of 340 passengers survived a crossing from the Netherlands to Pennsylvania. The others had starved to death.

For those who survived the transatlantic crossing, the relocation was just as traumatic. For centuries immigrants arrived in America with only a few distorted ideas about what life was like here. Many were desperate; they did not care what lay waiting for them because they had to leave their homes. Others had no way of obtaining detailed information about the land or its people. In 1848 Anne De Vrees, a seven year old from the Friesland province of Holland, believed that "the West" was the name of a large American city and many years later wrote about emigrating to America: "When we first beheld New York we were saying to each other, 'America is white!' We did not realize it was snow that gave the city this appearance, for it was winter and December 23."

During the 19th century, when most immigration to America occurred, many high hopes of instant happiness in America were quickly dashed. Although some immigrants eventually achieved their dreams of owning

land, building a home, or starting a business, they all had to deal with initial hardships. But the Dutch were luckier than most ethnic groups. Those who immigrated to America in the 19th century were unusually well organized. They arrived in groups and systematically researched the places they considered settling in. When they disembarked from their voyage in New York City, as most of them did, they received substantial help from the established Dutch of the area, who had been living there for 200 years.

*A Dutch mother travels with her 11 children to Minnesota in 1908.*

## Who Are the Dutch?

In the 1980 census, 6 million Americans claimed some Dutch descent. This may sound like a lot, but the number requires explanation. First, it is dwarfed in comparison to the 50 million people who listed themselves as "English" in the same census. Second, most of the 6 million people who called themselves "Dutch" cited that nationality as only one of several ethnic groups in

*In 1924 Dutch Americans celebrate Christmas together at the Holland-American club in Minneapolis.*

their background because the Dutch often married into French, Irish, German, and Scottish families producing children of mixed heritage. Third, the word *Dutch* can be interpreted in several ways.

In Europe, *Dutch* refers to citizens of the United Kingdom of the Netherlands, including inhabitants of Friesland province, who claim a long and proud cultural history separate from that of the Dutch. The label *Dutch* is also applied to a Flemish-speaking ethnic minority within neighboring Belgium. The confusion about Dutch identity also touches upon Dutch-speaking Germans who come from Grafschap Bentheim, a German province bordering the Netherlands. These men and women do not consider themselves members of the Dutch community.

Although all these peoples shared little in common in Europe, once in America they tended to put aside their differences. Nearly all of these ethnic subgroups lived together and intermarried in the Michigan Dutch communities of the 19th century, even if they began by founding separate towns when they first arrived. But problems of naming persisted in America. The well-known Pennsylvania Dutch, for example, are not actually Dutch at all, but German. The closeness of the two languages (*Deutsch* is the German word for *German*) led to a confusion of the two peoples. Even with all of these diverse definitions of Dutchness, the 6 million Americans who called themselves Dutch amount to only 3 percent of the total number of people polled in the 1980 census.

Like many other ethnic groups, the Dutch remained a close-knit and closed community within the diversity of American society until the start of the 20th century, when their settlements were swallowed up into rapidly expanding American suburbs. The Dutch gradually created a unique mixture of American and Dutch customs by which to live. Thus, as some of the earliest pioneers in U.S. history, they contributed to another national history as well as to their own. ∾

*In the 1670s Dutch artist Jacob van Ruisdael depicted his native city in* Panoramic View of the Amstel River Looking Toward Amsterdam.

# THE DUTCH HOMELAND

The nation known as Holland has long played a pivotal role in European history. This small, densely settled country has been entangled in so many conflicts and historic movements that its own chronology sometimes proves difficult to trace—as does the evolution of its name. Before 1648 the Dutch homeland was united with its southern neighbors, Belgium and Luxembourg. The three regions—although distinct in language and culture—composed a single economic and political unit known as the Netherlands or the Low Countries because they lay close to sea level.

In 1648 the Dutch splintered off to form the Republic of the United Provinces of the Netherlands. Since then the Netherlands has referred only to the Dutch homeland, commonly called Holland. In fact, Holland was actually the name of one of the original 7 (now 11) provinces that compose the United Provinces of the Netherlands. Holland (now divided into North and South Holland)—which contains the cities of Amsterdam, The Hague, and Rotterdam—commands such importance that foreigners have frequently confused it with the country as a whole.

Today the Netherlands occupies approximately 15,770 square miles along the northwestern coast of Europe. Nearly 40 percent of the country falls below sea level and remains dry through a complex system of

dunes, dikes, and drains—all designed to protect its densely populated terrain from the ever encroaching tides of the surrounding North Sea; in fact, its land has been overrun by foreigners as often as it has been inundated by floods.

## Roman Rule and the Middle Ages

In 55 B.C. Roman general Julius Caesar led the first military invasion of the region occupied by the Low Countries. He called the land Gallia Belgica and its inhabitants—peoples of either Celtic, Germanic, or Gallic descent—the Belgae. Even as he conquered them, Caesar praised the Belgae as a "most courageous" people in a written account of his campaigns in Gallia Belgica, *Commentaries on the Gallic Wars.*

By A.D. 300, Roman legions had abandoned Gallia Belgica, driven out by subsequent invasions launched by Germanic tribes. First came the Batavi, ancestors of the Dutch, next the Saxons, who also overran England, and finally the Franks. The Franks maintained control of the area from A.D. 600 until the death of their emperor, Charlemagne (Charles the Great), in 814. Charlemagne's three grandsons squabbled over the Low Countries in the aftermath of his death and divided the territory among themselves in the Treaty of Verdun, signed in 843.

By the Middle Ages (c. 500–1500) the Netherlands consisted of a loose union of small duchies, church lands, and independent towns. Because of their proximity to both the ocean and the inland, the Dutch were able to develop a thriving textile industry, first importing wool from England and Spain, then weaving it into cloth, which they sold to neighboring European countries. Commercial centers such as Amsterdam and Rotterdam often enjoyed the privilege of self-government, which was bestowed by an aristocratic class that controlled nearly all of the land in the Low Countries. Noblemen granted charters to towns in exchange for a share of the capital generated by the profitable manufacturing industries.

*An illustration from the French edition of* Commentaries on the Gallic Wars, *printed in 1520.*

*This miniature from a medieval text depicts women spinning and weaving flax into cloth, a pursuit that transformed the Netherlands into a textile center during the Middle Ages.*

The newly settled towns of the Netherlands soon attracted thousands of peasants from the surrounding rural areas, who had heard of their prosperity. Dutch from remote hamlets flocked to booming coastal provinces such as Holland, Zeeland, and Friesland. Their abandonment of the countryside hastened the decline of agriculture within the region, one of the first on the continent to move from an agrarian to a commercial economy. The towns dotting northeastern Europe bred a new type of inhabitant, worldly merchants and independent artisans who organized into guilds. The guilds quickly grew from trade associations into governing bodies that dominated the political life of medieval Europe. In the Low Countries, the guilds formed the basis of the democracies of the 17th century, including the United Provinces of the Netherlands.

The rapid rise of industry was paralleled by a surge of growth within another force in Europe, the Catholic church, which had first gained a foothold in the Netherlands during Roman rule. Between A.D. 400 and 800, Christian missionaries worked steadily to convert most of the Dutch to Catholicism. By the 1300s the church had established itself as a central institution in the Netherlands, yet despite its vast wealth and influence, it never attained the heights of power it did in other regions of Europe, such as Italy and France. In time the grandeur of the Catholic church would inspire not awe but resentment in many northern Europeans, who came to view Catholicism as a corrupt and repressive religion.

## The Era of the Burgundies and Hapsburgs

The Catholic church was rivaled in its influence only by a formidable ruling clan, the dukes of Burgundy, from a region of eastern France. In 1384 Philip the Bold of Burgundy assumed control over the provinces of Flanders and Artois. By 1445 his grandson Duke Philip the Good had expanded the original claim to include all territory held by the modern nations of the Nether-

lands, Belgium, and Luxembourg. He ruled this vast holding from a central government, located in the Belgian city of Brussels.

Philip tried to unite the Low Countries into one nation by adopting a single currency, establishing agencies of justice and finance, and calling together representatives from all of the provinces to counsel him on matters that concerned the region as a whole. Although power was still concentrated in the single person of the duke, the provinces of the Low Countries established a common identity.

In 1477, the defeat of Philip's son Duke Charles the Bold in battle ended the Burgundian rule of the Low Countries. The great Burgundy family was joined to another European dynasty, the Hapsburgs, when Charles's daughter Mary married Maximilian of Austria. The alliance brought the Low Countries into the sway of the powerful Hapsburg family, who continued to centralize the government of the Low Countries and to bring it into conformity with the other European holdings in their empire.

During the 16th century the Low Countries prospered economically and culturally. The industries founded in the 1600s—some as early as the 14th century—flourished. Belgian textiles were prized throughout Europe, and Antwerp, now a province of Belgium, became an important center of finance for the entire continent. The region grew even more dynamic during the Renaissance, the blossoming of Western culture that originated in Italy during the 14th century and spread northward. During the 1500s, the artistic influence of the Renaissance first reached the Low Countries through coastal cities, in which a cosmopolitan popu-

*A detail from Pieter Brueghel's* Return of the Hunter, *painted in 1565.*

lace benefited from an influx of ideas from foreign countries. Successful businessmen encouraged the region's cultural growth by acting as private patrons to such brilliant artists as Flemish painter Pieter Brueghel. These gentlemen of commerce also invested in such endeavors as book printing and overseas exploration—an enterprise that would lead to the founding of Dutch colonies around the world.

Neighboring nations affected the Low Countries in religious as well as cultural matters. In 1517 in the German province of Saxony, a monk named Martin Luther nailed a list of 95 demands for reform (known as the Ninety-five Theses) within the Catholic church to a church door. Luther believed that individual worshipers found salvation not through good works—such as giving large sums of money, or tithes, to the church—but through a strong religious faith. In time, Luther broke completely from Catholicism and founded a dissident sect of Christianity, Protestantism. Luther attracted interest in the Low Countries, at that time controlled by Charles V, a Catholic Hapsburg ruler. Many inhabitants of the region wanted to break free of Charles's tyrannical rule and adopted Protestantism as a means of opposing their Catholic emperor.

In 1556 Charles abdicated his crown, and his son Philip II assumed control of Spain and the Low Countries. As Charles had confronted Luther's Protestant movement, Philip faced a challenge from an even more radical theologian, John Calvin, born in Geneva, Switzerland, in 1509. Calvin taught that faith was insufficient to guarantee salvation. He claimed that the will of God alone—not good works or even faith—determined who would be the elect, or saved, and who would be damned. During the 1540s, Calvin tried to found a government based solely on religious law and the Bible.

Many Europeans—especially those in the Low Countries—praised this radical approach to government. Calvin's influence extended as far as England, where a group of Protestants known as Puritans lived

*A woodcut depicts Martin Luther nailing his Ninety-five Theses to a church door.*

*A portrait of John Calvin painted during his lifetime.*

by a similar doctrine. Thus, the Puritans of England and the Calvinists of northern Europe shared many similar beliefs. This commonality would greatly aid 19th-century Dutch immigrants to North America, then controlled chiefly by colonists of British Protestant descent.

Philip II was as intolerant of Protestantism as his father had been. Raised in Spain, Philip was a devout Catholic and he rigorously opposed other religions. His rigidity pushed the Low Countries to the brink of revolt. The Dutch and their neighbors resented the oppression of the Catholic church and bridled at the rule of the Hapsburgs, foreigners who drained banks and businesses dry in order to finance their costly wars abroad.

In 1565 the Low Countries took action. Local aristocracy, wealthy merchants, and the oppressed rural and urban poor united in resistance to the Spanish rulers. William of Orange, a Calvinist prince from a northern province, became the first leader of an 80-year struggle for independence and religious tolerance. Although William himself was killed by a Catholic assassin in 1584, what the Dutch call the Eighty Year War ultimately succeeded in its aims. In 1648 the northern provinces of the Low Countries gained official recognition as the Republic of the United Provinces of the Netherlands, while the southern region remained the Spanish Netherlands, later Belgium and Luxembourg.

Their victory against the Spanish led directly to other triumphs for the Dutch. They now focused their energies on repairing the ravages of war and on enjoying the civilized pleasures of peacetime. During the 17th century, the Netherlands enjoyed a golden age of achievement in art, trade, industry, exploration, and science. The port of Amsterdam grew into a thriving international metropolis with tolerant local laws that attracted Jews, Huguenots (French Protestants), Puritans, and other religious refugees. Through their mastery of the sea, the Dutch founded and financed an immense colonial empire.

HAERLEM.

During the 1600s, Amsterdam merchants founded the Dutch East India Company and its counterpart, the Dutch West India Company. The two enterprises fostered trade internationally and established Dutch colonies all over the map. For a brief time, the Dutch boasted holdings in North and South America, South Africa, the Caribbean, and Indonesia. Dutch traders dealt in slaves, spices, and fur. Although they soon lost their North American colony, New Netherland, their Eastern empire was a longtime source of wealth.

Political independence and economic prosperity brought new problems to the Netherlands. Dutch leaders faced a dilemma concerning the form of government they would adopt. They finally agreed that the seven

*A 16th-century engraving depicts Spanish troops massacring citizens of Haarlem, the Netherlands, during the Dutch war of independence against Spain.*

*A painting shows the States-General of the Netherlands assembled in 1651.*

provinces composing the Netherlands should be ruled by a legislative body called the States-General. Members of the legislature were required to reach a consensus on all decisions they made. Strife soon developed and pitted two factions of the States-General against each other: those who argued for the supremacy of the national government over the individual provinces, and those who asserted the independence of the provinces and the importance of local rule. The latter group contained families of Dutch aristocrats who had handed down their privilege and influence from one generation to the next. This elite class resisted the idea of a central government because they feared the loss of their hereditary privileges. In time the feud between the groups would intensify and weaken the United Provinces of the Netherlands, making the young nation prey to foreign domination.

## The Coming of Napoleon

During the latter half of the 17th century, England replaced Spain as the preeminent power in Europe. The Dutch sometimes found themselves in competition with the English, who also raced to establish colonies in the New World territory in North America. Sometimes the conflict between the two countries erupted into warfare, as in 1664 when the British conquered New Netherland. But before the end of the century the rival nations were forced into an alliance in order to counter the growing aggression of another European power, France.

Louis XIV, the dynamic and ambitious king of France, was crowned in 1643 and from then until his death in 1715 occupied center stage in European politics, building his native country into a formidable power. Between the late 1600s and 1795 the French occupied northeastern Europe three times, finally launching a full-scale invasion of the Netherlands in 1795, just six years after their own government had been rocked by revolution.

Under the direction of a brilliant French commander named Napoleon Bonaparte, military forces instituted a series of drastic reforms designed to reorganize the government of the Netherlands and impose upon it the ideals of the French Revolution. Na-

*Prince William V of Orange was forced to flee his homeland in 1794, when the French army overran the Netherlands.*

poleon stripped the Calvinists' Dutch Reformed church of much of its power, established a new code of law, minted new coins, and set up a new system of weights and measures. He even renamed the Dutch homeland, calling it the Batavian Republic.

The Dutch resented this intrusion into their nation. In 1806 their country was absorbed into the expanding French Empire when Napoleon installed his brother Louis Bonaparte as king of the Netherlands from 1806 to 1810. After Louis was removed, other Frenchmen ran the country until 1813, when the forces of Europe joined to defeat Napoleon. In 1815 a postwar council of European leaders met in Vienna and united the Netherlands and Belgium into a single independent nation, the Kingdom of the Netherlands, ruled by King William I, son of William V of Orange, a descendant of the House of Orange.

The union of the Protestant, Dutch-speaking Netherlands with predominantly Catholic, French-speaking Belgium proved ill-fated and lasted only 15 years, until 1830. But during that time the Dutch benefited from Belgium's greater prosperity. Throughout the preceding 50 years the Belgians had steadily industrialized, producing coal and manufactured goods for export. In contrast, the Netherlands was still paralyzed by poverty and disorder—the result of the tumultuous wars and occupations of the 18th century. The countryside, not yet recovered from stampedes of foreign soldiers, suffered an agricultural depression.

But as before in their history, the Dutch displayed a remarkable ability for both political and economic achievement. They created new and successful industries while modernizing old ones, and in 1848 they wrote a constitution and instituted a new form of government, a parliamentary monarchy modeled after that of Great Britain. Thus, like England, the Netherlands was guided by both a regent and an elected parliament. The Dutch enjoyed great stability from the mid-1800s until the turn of the century. As in the great age of the

1600s, the newly resurrected nation enjoyed an era of cultural innovation.

No figure better personifies that golden era than Postimpressionist painter Vincent van Gogh. Born in the Netherlands in 1853, van Gogh enjoyed little fame during his lifetime but in time commanded a worldwide reputation for his paintings, which were characterized by a heightened use of color and bold, slashlike brush stokes. His beautiful and disturbing works also vividly portray the artist's often agitated state of mind. Van Gogh's suicide in 1890 prematurely ended his life, but his works stand as a testament to his genius and his emotional torment.

*In 1882 Vincent van Gogh painted* Women Miners, *one of several works about the daily lives of impoverished country dwellers.*

## The Two World Wars

By 1914, when all of Europe was convulsed by World War I, the Dutch were caught in the crossfire between Germany and its enemies, Britain and France. The Netherlands—because it declared itself neutral—was spared the mass destruction of its male population, a devastation borne by other European nations. Nonetheless, the Dutch suffered financial losses, food shortages, and civil unrest. Just as they withstood the despair of wartime, the Dutch reveled in the euphoria enjoyed by all of Europe during the 1920s, a time of global prosperity. During that decade they completed ambitious engineering projects to control flooding and reclaim land for farming. At the end of the 1920s, however, a worldwide economic depression occurred, plunging all of Europe, including the Netherlands, into poverty throughout the 1930s. But the government was quick to implement relief measures, so the Dutch were well off in comparison to the rest of the world.

*Anne Frank sent this photograph of herself to an American pen pal in 1942. The inscription reads: "This photo shows me as I would always like to appear. Maybe then I could go to Hollywood."*

Dit is een foto, zoals ik me zou wensen, altijd zo te zijn. Dan had ik nog wel een kans om naar Holywood te komen. Anne Frank. 10 Oct. 1942

The misery of impoverishment was soon intensified by the agony of World War II. On May 10, 1940, the Nazi German leader Hitler's troops invaded the Netherlands and subdued it in five days. The occupation lasted five long years, during which the Dutch endured bombings and severe shortages of food and fuel. But such inconveniences—although a threat to the populace—paled in the face of the mass slaughter of 110,000 Dutch Jews, who were deported to death camps throughout Eastern Europe. The plight of Dutch Jews was detailed by Anne Frank, a young Jewish girl who documented her last years in Holland before being discovered and deported. (Frank later died in a concentration camp.) Her diary, which she addressed as "Kitty," reveals the brave efforts of an adolescent girl to retain her courage and hope while her family—in hiding with a gentile family—is hunted down by Nazi troops. As Frank's diary suggests, Jews depended on, and received, the aid of many of their gentile neighbors, who sheltered and protected Jews or lightened their desperation with gifts and visits.

In the spring of 1945 Allied troops liberated Europe from German domination, yet many of the hardships brought on by the war lingered into peacetime. Mass food shortages, for example, continued for several years because much of the valuable farming land had been destroyed by flooding during the occupation. In 1948, the United States provided timely assistance in the form of the Marshall Plan, which designated to the Netherlands and other bankrupt countries funds for rebuilding domestic industries and repairing war damage. The effects of World War II deprived the Dutch of most of their remaining colonies after the war; the country retained Indonesia and Suriname only until 1954.

In the postwar era problems of overcrowding, urbanization, inflation, and resource management afflicted the Netherlands, yet in general the country emerged a stable and prosperous one after the traumas of the early 20th century. ～

*A structure topped with cubes typifies the innovative architecture of postwar Amsterdam.*

An engraving from a book
shows Peter Minuit buying
Manhattan from its native
inhabitants.

# NEW NETHERLAND, 1609–64

To describe minutely the gradual advances, from the rude
log hut, to the stately dutch mansion, with a brick front,
glass windows, and shingle roof—from the tangled thicket,
to the luxuriant cabbage garden . . . would probably be
fatiguing to my reader, and certainly very inconvenient to
myself; suffice it to say, trees were cut down, stumps
grubbed up, bushes cleared away, until the new city rose
gradually from amid swamps and stinkweeds, like a mighty
fungus, springing from a mass of rotten wood.

—Washington Irving on the growth of New Amsterdam,
from *A History of New York from the Beginning of the World
to the End of the Dutch Dynasty.*

The history of New Netherland began in 1609
when the Dutch East India Company contracted
British explorer Henry Hudson to find a new
route to China. In March of that year, Hudson set sail
from Amsterdam in his ship the *Half Moon.* Although
he failed to find the desired course to the East that he
had hoped to discover by sailing northwest, he did discover the New York river and, later, the Canadian bay
that now bear his name. He claimed them for the Dutch
East India Company. By 1614 the company had in-
creased its North American holdings to include a vast
territory stretching from the Connecticut River to the
Delaware River. The area was named New Netherland.

TOTIUS NEOBELGII NOVA ET ACCURATISSIMA TABULA.

*New Netherland appears in a 17th-century Dutch map of the New World.*

The Dutch founded New Netherland in order to enter into the profitable fur trade. They were aided in this venture both by local abundance of beaver—by far the most coveted fur in Europe—and by the prime location of their colony. The Hudson River offered easy access to the interior of the colony and a convenient outlet to the Atlantic Ocean. But New Netherland's central position on the East Coast proved a detriment as well as an advantage. Nestled between two expanding British colonies, New England and Maryland, New Netherland was vulnerable to the encroachment of English colonists, who greatly outnumbered the Dutch.

News of the new colony quickly spread throughout Amsterdam, where in 1621 a group of businessmen chartered the Dutch West India Company—a counterpart of the Dutch East India Company—in order to conduct trade in the New World. The new company cornered the North American fur trade and quickly grew into a powerful force in the region. But the colony lacked inhabitants until 1624, when the first Dutch settlers—about 30 families and a handful of single men— arrived in North America, sponsored by the Dutch West India Company. The company provided the immigrants with ships, crews, and necessities such as building materials, tools, and livestock. These forebears of Dutch Americans established their first homesteads on the Hudson River at Fort Orange, near what is now the city of Albany, New York.

The earliest homesteads amounted to no more than primitive shelters, carved out of holes in the ground. Immigrants dug a seven- or eight-foot hole, lined it with twigs and tree bark, and covered the top with a makeshift roof. As the settlements became more permanent later on in the century, the Dutch built brick houses whenever possible, although bricks were scarce in the colony. These orderly dwellings, which bespoke the Dutch reputation for neatness and cleanliness, were often fronted by porches enclosed by wooden roofs and lattice work. They were kept very neat and clean, with whitewashed walls and built-in furniture.

## A Rough Beginning

So many aspects of the settlers' lives were controlled by the Dutch West India Company that the trading enterprise began to assume a second role: that of governing the colony. The dual responsibilities of business and government often conflicted with one another because the best interests of the colonists and those of the company's backers in Amsterdam often differed. As the New World territory grew, the company had to decide whether its first loyalty lay with its investors in Amsterdam or with the Dutch peopling the colony. In the end the company sided with its investors.

The colonists resented playing second fiddle to overseas investors, however, and demanded that the company expend some of its profits on their well-being. For example, they demanded military protection from the threat of Indian attack, sufficient supplies of food and manufactured goods, and orderly management. But the Dutch West India Company often failed to fulfill the colonists' diverse demands, and as a result the colonists complained endlessly about their plight.

Their grievances often focused on the haphazard form of government offered by the company, which charged various ship captains with the responsibilities of leadership. In 1626 the Dutch West India Company appeased the settlers by appointing a permanent governor general for New Netherland, Peter Minuit. Just after his appointment, Minuit bought the island of Manhattan from a local native tribe for $24 and built a fort to guard the entrance to the harbor, making the island town of New Amsterdam the headquarters of New Netherland. His purchase proved a timely one. In 1626–28 the colonists found themselves caught in the crossfire of war between the Mohegan and Mohawk Indians and were driven from Fort Orange southward to New Amsterdam.

After securing Manhattan Island for the Dutch, Minuit turned his attention to the unenviable job of organizing the hodgepodge band of colonists in New Amsterdam into a civilized society and the colony into a successful business enterprise. When Minuit assumed office he faced two obstacles to these goals: the scarcity of settlers and the rough—and even criminal—nature of the people who willingly journeyed to the colony. The vast majority of Dutch had no desire to leave their homeland, which enjoyed a golden age during the 1600s, and risk their life on a long sea crossing in order to settle in a strange wilderness. Thus, the Dutch West India Company could barely recruit enough settlers to

*An artist's depiction of Henry Hudson aboard the* Half Moon *in New York Harbor.*

populate New Netherland, and once they arrived the immigrants were often loath to stay. The majority of those who did remain had been on the fringes of European society: religious refugees, beggars, revolutionaries, adventurers, and even criminals—those who were attracted to life at a frontier trading post.

## The Patroon System

The scant population of the colony proved a serious problem. The traders could not survive without a supporting community of builders, farmers, tailors, doctors, ministers, cobblers, and soldiers. Instead, colonists had to import goods and services from the Netherlands. In 1629, in response to this mounting crisis, the Dutch West India Company devised a new plan to entice more people to the colony. The company agreed to loosen its hold on the fur trade and allow certain wealthy Dutchmen, called *patroons*, to buy land and establish their own private estates, where they could organize communities without any supervision and retain the profits reaped from fishing and hunting, growing crops, and trading furs. In exchange for these

*Stephen van Rensselaer,
Kiliaen's son, poses for a
portrait painted in about 1730.*

privileges, the patroons were each required to lure 50 new settlers to New Netherland.

Three patroonships, as they were called, were quickly established. Swanendael, a small Dutch community in Delaware; Pavonia, in New Jersey; and Rensselaerswyck, located north of New Amsterdam. The first two settlements were destroyed by Indian attacks soon after their founding, but the third, which comprised several hundred thousand acres, flourished. The city of Rensselaer, New York, still stands today. The founder of Rensselaerswyck, Kiliaen van Rensselaer, took great pains with his lands, appointing able managers and supervising their work closely. As patroon, he wielded enormous authority over the lives of the settlers: He administered justice, chose which crops could be planted, and regulated trade. The patroonships experienced many of the same problems as the colony as a whole, but on a smaller scale. In the end the patroon plan achieved success in Rensselaerswyck but did little to solve the population problem of New Netherland.

The plight of New Netherland came to the attention of the States-General, the national governing body of the Netherlands. This legislature focused its attention on two problems: that of peopling the Dutch colony and that of guaranteeing its security against hostile invaders from the British colony of New England. In 1639 the Dutch government forced the Dutch West India Company to end its monopoly on the fur trade in order to encourage migration to North America. The plan yielded immediate results. Dutch arrived in the colony in greater numbers, drawn by hopes of getting rich from the trade in beaver and other furs.

Yet even the greater number of colonists arriving proved insufficient to fill the barren wilderness with settlements, as was desired. During the mid-1600s, most of the region, with the exception of New Amsterdam, was a dangerous territory, beset by attacks from local Indian tribes. During the 1640s, for example, Dutch settlers continually battled with the Algonquian

Indians. In 1645 the two sides declared peace, but the calm was broken again in 1647 when the new governor-general, Peter Stuyvesant, renewed the conflict.

## Peter Stuyvesant

A soldier by training, Stuyvesant governed the colony with an iron hand. By 1649 his authoritarian method of leadership aroused so much resentment that one New Amsterdam resident, Adriaen Van der Donck, sent a formal complaint to the Dutch government, asking it to remove the Dutch West India Company from control of the colony.

In particular, colonists objected to Stuyvesant's suppression of religions other than his own, Calvinism. The Dutch Reformed Church of America had been founded in New Netherland in 1628 and during the colonial era it operated under the supervision of the mother church in the Netherlands. But despite the conservatism of the church and of men like Stuyvesant, New Amsterdam showed extreme tolerance to any number of religious refugees who had flocked to the colony, including Walloons (French-speaking Protestants from the southern provinces of the Netherlands), Jews from Portugal and its colony, Brazil, and Dutch Catholics—all those who felt at home neither in their native land nor in the Calvinist Netherlands.

Perhaps because of the great religious diversity of settlers, New Netherland inhabitants practiced almost none of the Calvinist ethics of industriousness, sobriety, and devotion to God. In 1648 a New Amsterdam survey estimated that one out of four city businesses was a tavern. In 1656, in reaction to the rowdiness of city dwellers, New Amsterdam officials posted a law forbidding many activities on the Sabbath, including "any ordinary labor, such as Ploughing, Sowing, Mowing, Building, Woodsawing, Smithing, Bleaching, Hunting [and] Fishing" as well as "frequenting Taverns or Tippling Houses, Dancing, playing Ball, Cards, Trick-

*In about 1660 Peter Stuyvesant sat for this work by an unknown artist, one of the earliest portraits in American history.*

*In a work by Dutch artist Jacob Duck, Dutchmen in New Amsterdam play ninepins, a game imported to the colony from the Netherlands.*

track, Tennis, Cricket or Ninepins [and] going on pleasure parties in a Boat, Cart or Wagon. . . ." In 1663 city officials broadened the ordinance to include "roving in search of Nuts or strawberries and . . . too much unrestrained and excessive Playing, Shouting, and Screaming of children in the Streets and Highways." Despite Calvinist bans, the Dutch in the New World enjoyed horseracing, golf, sleighing, skating, and smoking. In addition to boisterous frontier people, the colonies did attract some sober citizens: businessmen, soldiers, ministers, merchants, farmers, artisans, and even some artists. Most New Netherland painters had received their training on the European continent. At times they supplemented the income made from painting portraits by working at glassmaking, house painting, trade, and farming. The list of 17th-century Dutch painters in New Amsterdam includes Jacobus Gerritsen Strycker, Evert Duyckinck, and Hendrik Couturier.

The vast majority of colonists engaged themselves not with art but with agriculture. Farming became increasingly important to the life of the colony. The Dutch were enthusiastic farmers because the scarcity of farmland in the Netherlands made farming a prestigious employment. As the colony developed, the Dutch moved from the two ports, New Amsterdam and Fort Orange, to the fertile lands that banked the Hudson River in order to till the soil there. Washington Irving, the early-19th-century New York writer and historian, frequently wrote about the Dutch and their communities in the Hudson Valley. He caricatured New World Dutch farmers in his most famed work of fiction, *The Legend of Sleepy Hollow*:

> Old Baltus Van Tassel was a perfect picture of a thriving, contented, liberal hearted farmer. He seldom, it is true, sent either his eyes or his thoughts beyond the boundaries of his own farm; but within those every thing was snug, happy, and well conditioned. He was satisfied with his wealth, but not proud of it, and piqued himself upon the hearty abundance, rather than the style in which he lived.

Yet even this movement toward farming did not fulfill the growing need for food within New Netherland. In 1658 Peter Stuyvesant responded to the demand for crops by organizing a special agricultural community called Nieuw Haarlem (today the neigh-

*Washington Irving's stories of the colonial Dutch inspired* The Return of Rip Van Winkle, *by American painter John Quidor.*

borhood of Harlem in New York City), located on the northern tip of Manhattan island. Farmers who relocated to Harlem were loaned land that they could purchase over a period of three years while farming it.

The colony continued to slowly expand and even developed a thriving trade with other East Coast colonies, but New Netherland was still plagued by fundamental problems of underpopulation and—as the States-General had feared and predicted—the encroachment of British colonials, who far outnumbered their Dutch counterparts. In 1664 the total population of New Netherland equaled approximately 10,000, whereas that of New England neared 50,000.

The British were so skeptical of the Dutch West India Company's ability to successfully defend its claim to New Netherland that on March 22, 1664, King Charles II of England gave New Netherland to his brother, the duke of York, as a gift. Washington Irving commented on Charles II's gesture in *A History of New York*: "None but great monarchs have a right to give away what does not belong to them."

The Dutch expressed outrage when they learned about the British monarch's actions. On August 28, 1664, the threat of takeover became a reality when British forces took over the colony with barely a struggle.

*This engraving shows Peter Stuyvesant's surrender of New Amsterdam.*

On September 5 of that year New Netherland surrendered, becoming the British colony of New York. Fort Orange was renamed Albany, New Amsterdam became New York City, and countless other Dutch place-names were anglicized. Although the Dutch reclaimed their colony for a few months in 1673, their brief experiment in establishing a North American empire had ended.

In 1665 Peter Stuyvesant reported to the States-General about the loss of New Netherland. He complained about the lack of soldiers, asserting that the 300 able-bodied men at his service could not successfully defend the colony against the onslaught of British troops: The Dutch lacked gunpowder, food, and other essential provisions. And the fort at New Amsterdam lay in a state of disorder, with cattle roaming around the premises. Finally, Stuyvesant wrote: "In addition to the want of the above-mentioned necessaries, and many other minor articles, a general discontent and unwillingness to assist in defending the place became man-

*A view of Fort George in the city of New York in about 1735, approximately 70 years after the English took over New Netherland.*

ifest among the people." Although the governor had summoned Dutchmen from the farms surrounding New Amsterdam, few had agreed to leave their land at harvest time and fewer still enlisted to defend the colony.

Stuyvesant knew that the British discouraged the Dutch from volunteering for military service. The British had shrewdly exploited the Dutch colonists' dissatisfaction with the Dutch West India Company, issuing open letters in which they guaranteed that the Dutch could keep their property under British rule. In addition, the British promised that the Dutch would enjoy unrestricted trade with Holland and England and in time would prove lenient rulers of New York's Dutch community. This final provision convinced wealthy New Amsterdam merchants and other prominent citizens of the colony to yield to British rule:

> If the Honorable Company give themselves so little concern about the safety of the country and its inhabitants as not to be willing to send a ship of war to its succor in such pressing necessity, nor even a letter of advice as to what we may depend on and what succor we have to expect, we are utterly powerless, and, therefore, not bound to defend the city to imperil our lives, property, wives, and children without hope of any succor or relief, and to lose all after two or three days' resistance.

In his *History of New York*, Irving offered another interpretation of New Netherland's history: "The guileless government of the New Netherlands . . . like a worthy unsuspicious old burgher, quietly settled itself down into the city of New Amsterdam, as into a snug elbow chair—and fell into a comfortable nap—while in the meantime cunning neighbors stepp'd in and picked its pockets."

The company's neglect had taken its toll. The Dutch West India Company suffered, in the end, by mistreating the very colonists they had wooed to North America. Yet the company alone did not bring about the demise of New Netherland. Many Dutch refused to settle permanently in North America because the wilderness of the New World seemed especially harsh compared to the comforts afforded by Europe.

Although England's invasion brought the Dutch colony to an end and virtually halted all immigration from the Netherlands, the British gave lenient treatment to the Dutch who chose to remain in New York. Without a colony of countrymen to sustain them, however, the Dutch in the New World began to lose contact with their native culture, especially the Dutch language. According to writer and editor H. L. Mencken:

> . . . the English tried to wipe out Dutch [language] in New York after the conquest of the colony in 1664, but it carried on an underground existence for many years, and so late as the second half of the 18th century an English observer was reporting that it was "still so much used in some counties that the sheriffs find it difficult to obtain persons sufficiently acquainted with the English tongue to serve as jurors in the courts of law." Dutch, indeed, was the first language in some of the remoter parts of the Hudson valley until [the 20th century], and also in parts of New Jersey.

Although Dutch eventually died out, American English still contains many remnants of the language, including the words *cookie*, *spook*, and *waffle*. In fact, Mencken believed that the classic Americanism, *Yankee*, was originally a Dutch nickname for Dutch seamen. If American phrases using the word *Dutch* (such as speaking *double Dutch*, or gibberish) often seem to degrade the Dutch it is because these expressions were coined by Englishmen who competed with Dutch merchants.

The British conquest of New Netherland effectively squelched Dutch culture, but the takeover closed only the first chapter of the history of the Dutch in North America. Within 200 years the next wave of emigration from Holland arrived on U.S. shores, bringing a new generation of Dutch to the New World. ∿

*This 18th-century American portrait of Susan and William Van Voorhis Rapalje, the children of early Dutch Americans, was painted in the English style popularized by the British artist Thomas Gainsborough.*

# THE DUTCH IN THE MIDWEST, 1840s–1880s

After seven long weeks on the sea . . . we finally arrived in New York. Speedily we noted that we were in a strange land where everything seemed odd to us, but also that we ourselves were looked upon as a very strange kind of people." With these words Egbert Frederiks recounted the beginning of his new life in America. In 1846 Frederiks fled religious persecution and economic hardship in the Netherlands in order to emigrate to America. He was one of the first of a great migration of 19th-century Dutch immigrants who left their homes for the uncertain prospects of frontier life in America.

Between 1840 and the beginning of the American Civil War in 1861 approximately 20,000 Dutch packed their belongings and set out for North America. Most of them, like Egbert Frederiks, came from rural regions of the Netherlands. After settling in America, these religious refugees were joined by a great migration of nearly 230,000 impoverished peasants and artisans, who flowed into the country until the turn of the century. These country dwellers were driven overseas by a series of dramatic events that altered the course of European history and, ultimately, that of the United States, as well.

*On January 19, 1795, the French army entered Amsterdam.*

The Napoleonic Wars, which swept through Europe from approximately 1803 to 1815, crippled the Netherlands. Foreign soldiers overran the Low Countries and left the Netherlands with the triple blight of high unemployment, growing poverty, and an agricultural crisis. At one time the countryside had been drained of salt water in order to make the soil arable, but the land had been ruined by floods that entered the low-lying areas when dikes and dams were destroyed during battles. Rural areas suffered, too, from a scourge that killed livestock by the hundreds and a pestilence that infested the potato crop. Onto this background of hunger and despair emerged the religious conflict that, coupled with economic hardship, drove so many Dutch from their homeland.

Throughout the early 1800s the Dutch government exerted increasing control over the official church of the nation, the Dutch Reformed church. Like many other European governments, that of the Netherlands increasingly fell under the influence of the Enlightenment—an 18th-century philosophical movement that advocated, among other things, the separation of church and state. When the Netherlands restructured its administration after the Napoleonic Wars, it allocated to the government power and authority that had traditionally fallen within the domain of the Dutch Reformed church. For example, the government began to oversee the training and supervision of the clergy. Many Dutch, especially orthodox Calvinists, bitterly objected to the intrusion of secular officials into the life of the church.

In 1834 several Dutch Reformed church ministers (or, in Dutch, *dominies*) pitted themselves against the new church hierarchy. Albertus Van Raalte, Hendrik Scholte, Anthony Brummelkamp, and their congregations formally seceded from the Dutch Reformed church in protest. The state responded by persecuting the group with fines, imprisonment, and abuses. In the words of one man, son of a prominent dissident dominie: "Insulting names were given them. . . . Those in business lost their customers. Wage earners were dismissed." This treatment served only to harden their resolve to emigrate to a land where they could practice the Dutch Reformed faith without interference. By 1840, when the state stopped persecuting the seceders, many rural communities in Holland had already decided to emigrate together to America.

## An Orderly Exodus

From its beginnings, the migration of the Dutch to America differed from that of most other groups in its orderliness. Even before actually embarking on their journey across the Atlantic, the Dutch worked hard to organize themselves. Before deciding to leave emigrants generally consulted with their families, friends, and ministers. Their leaders raised funds, recruited settlers, and educated themselves about life in the New World as thoroughly as possible.

They also rekindled ties with Dutch already living in America, the descendants of the original New Netherland colonists. In May 1846, for example, Van Raalte and Brummelkamp wrote an "Appeal to the Faithful

*A mural in the post office of Pella, Iowa—a town founded by Dutch colonists—memorializes the journey of Dutch immigrants to North America.*

in the United States in North America," an open letter to the Dutch congregations in America that would aid the individual settlers by enabling them to initially settle with friends and relatives.

Potential emigrants also organized associations based on regional background, common religious beliefs, and shared aspirations for their life in the new country. They established charters to begin new communities in America and left home with a precise idea of where they wanted to settle and why. Because most emigrants intended to farm, many associations sent out advance scouting parties to investigate the quality of farmland available in various parts of the United States.

Late in September 1846 Dominie Van Raalte sailed from the province of Holland with more than 100 members of his congregation, including Egbert Frederiks. The long crossing caused sickness and took several lives, including that of Egbert Frederiks's young son. Once they arrived in New York, the group was welcomed by congregants of the Dutch Reformed Church of America. Appeals for assistance, published in the church's newsletter, *The Christian Intelligencer*, brought forth generous donations and letters of support from many established Dutch Americans.

On November 26, 1846, the *Intelligencer* published an unsigned response to the open letter Van Raalte had sent from overseas just six months before:

Now I might say, and would say, in behalf of all the faithful [Dutch], to these Christian people: Come on friends. Though we have no money to bestow, we can direct you to suitable locations, give employment to your mechanics, furnish land for your farmers to cultivate till they get land of their own, and aid you in various ways, so as to make your circumstances comfortable, and expedite those important objects you have in view in leaving your native country.

## Holland, Michigan

Van Raalte's group pressed on from New York, intending to settle in Wisconsin, attracted by its gently rolling hills and abundance of farmland. En route the Dutch newcomers stopped in Albany and Buffalo, hurrying on to Detroit by steamer. The Detroit Dutch dissuaded their compatriots from their original plans and convinced them to stay in Michigan. There Van Raalte and his contingent purchased 1,000 tree-filled acres in the western part of the state, calling this new settlement Holland, after the Dutch province they had once called home.

Living conditions were primitive, and the immigrants suffered a mortality rate of almost 50 percent. The local swamps bred malaria, and the area lacked roads or even clearings. The Dutch were forced to perform the backbreaking labor of clearing the land of trees—a skill that they had to learn on the spot because the farmland in Europe had long been cleared. One Dutchman, naively confident that he could cut down any tree, destroyed a new house when the tree fell in the wrong direction. And once the trees had been cut, their stumps and root systems were often left, the pioneers feeling it was easier to cultivate their crops amid these remains than to remove the stumps.

Life in Michigan failed to improve by the summer of 1847, when Engbertus Van Der Veen and his family joined Van Raalte's group. In fact, the Van Der Veens were so shocked by the state of the Holland settlement that they refused to unpack their luggage, leaving trunks and boxes on the beach of Lake Michigan in the hope that a ship would stop and rescue them. Engbertus

*A portrait of Albertus van Raalte, a founding father of Holland, Michigan.*

*This log cabin built by Dutch-American settlers still stands in Holland, Michigan.*

Van Der Veen reported that fresh meat was so scarce in the new colony that when a supply ship anchored offshore with stores of such luxuries as meat, everyone scrambled to greet it. But because meat was in short supply, it was sold first to the sick. Everyone else, says Engbertus Van Der Veen, "went home happy that they had actually seen fresh meat" and continued with their diet of corn, bread, and potatoes—frontier staples. Favorite dishes included *hutspot*, a combination of potatoes and cabbage, and *botermelk pap*, a soup concocted of barley and buttermilk boiled together and sweetened with brown sugar or syrup.

After two months in their new environment, the Van Der Veens resigned themselves to enduring the hardships of their new environment. They lived in a log cabin that Engbertus described as "a large birdcage because of the chinks between the logs and hemlock branches." The cabin, he also noted, leaked whenever it rained. Engbertus painted a vivid picture of life in that rustic dwelling:

> The table was placed in the center of the room; our beds were spread out on the ground for there was no floor. Water pitcher, bowls, plates, umbrellas, and other objects gave some impression of civilized life and reminded us somewhat of our life beyond the sea. Evening and night came as before and also the strange and unbearable variety of sounds. Again there was that horrid hooting and croaking. We placed an open umbrella in the door of our dwelling to keep any unlawful intruder, man or beast, from walking in.

*An immigrant family poses for a portrait in traditional Dutch dress.*

## Daily Life in the New Eden

The quarters were close in the Dutch settlement, and two or more families often shared the same two-room cabin. Some, lacking even this luxury, sheltered themselves instead in storage sheds or in lean-tos thrown together from twigs and bark. The Hollanders bravely tolerated these hardships and quickly grew adept at the new skills required of them on the frontier: They learned to fashion candles, make soap, spin, weave, and to cook on an open fire instead of a wood-burning stove. Survival was the main task, and Dutch of all ages participated in this effort. Teenagers, for example, traveled to distant towns to work for second- or third-generation Americans in order to earn pocket money for the whole family while their parents struggled to farm the land.

Such travails often took immigrants by surprise, because they arrived in America with mistaken expectations. In the Netherlands, Dutch farmers usually learned about pioneer existence through letters from family and friends that often glossed over the harsh daily realities. Occasionally, however, an immigrant would be so overwhelmed with the hardships of daily life that he or she would put pen to paper and communicate woes to family back in Europe: "Many a person had thought he was emigrating to an earthly paradise, a happy dreamland in America," one disillusioned immigrant wrote. "But now they beheld a wild waste, impenetrable woods, practically no fellow human beings, nor the least trace of farming or other activity, nor saw anywhere a house fit to live in."

Misinformation was also given in flyers distributed by professional speculators, who traveled through the European countryside trying to attract settlers to frontier areas. Many of these men resorted to unscrupulous business practices and wanted only to turn a profit by selling undesirable land to trusting emigrants. Their flyers distorted the reality of America and misled many Dutch men and women into thinking of the New World as "the promised land" depicted in their Bible.

*A depiction of the First Reformed Church in Holland, Michigan, founded in 1847.*

In fact, many potential immigrants seem to have associated the New World with biblical descriptions of paradise. Dutch accounts of America are full of religious references, especially to the promised land, Canaan. This is understandable considering the importance of religion in their reasons for leaving the Netherlands and in their lives. Adriaan Zwemer, who borrowed money to emigrate in 1849 and was then sponsored by his church to become a Dutch Reformed minister in America, wrote: "Letters written by earlier emigrants to that locality, some of which had been read in church, gave us the impression that the Western part of Michigan was like another Canaan—a land full of pious people and so far in the Western part of the world that evil had not yet penetrated there."

Sometimes this vision was borne out in reality. Engbertus Van Der Veen, for example, wrote warmly of life in Michigan once his family began to farm in earnest. Having dreamed of Amsterdam every night after first arriving, he soon felt proud of the progress of Holland, Michigan, and of the Dutch settlers' ability to transform the land from a bleak wilderness to a thriving village. By the end of the 1840s Holland boasted 200 houses, including painted frame dwellings with front yards and fragrant gardens. Several stores had been established by blacksmiths, tailors, shoemakers, and

*The campus of Hope College, an institution that still stands as testimony to the aspirations of Michigan's Dutch settlers.*

other artisans who sold their goods and services to the settlers.

## A Thriving Community

As the community developed, residents erected churches, paved roads, and in 1851 erected a secondary school, first called the Pioneer School and in 1855 renamed Holland Academy. In 1866 school officials added college-level courses to the curriculum, and the Holland Academy evolved into Hope College. The college gained nationwide recognition as an excellent liberal arts institution and as of 1988 still claimed an enrollment of several thousand students. However, Hope College was not the Dutch Americans' first institution of higher learning in the United States. That distinction goes to Rutgers College, established by colonists in Paterson, New Jersey, in 1766 (now a state university of the same name located in New Brunswick, New Jersey).

Outsiders who visited Holland, Michigan, during the 1850s marveled at the great strides made by the town and its residents. One American who lived in Holland, Michigan, for a few years beginning in 1854 admired the immaculate order of Dutch homes. Another commented on the newness of the town—with its sawdust- and sand-covered streets and its thick surrounding forests. In 1853 Holland's reputation spread farther when a journalist from the *New York Tribune* wrote a newpaper article in which he commented on the unity of its inhabitants: "The people have sufficient similarity of feeling and principle to act together as a body. They represent a large and influential class of the people of Holland, and retain a connection with them."

The newsman commended their ability to adjust to western life. He also lauded the Dutch as industrious, frugal, and persevering: This perception of the Dutch was shared by many in mainstream American society. Outsiders often attributed these virtues to the immigrants' strict Calvinism. Thus the Dutch established a reputation as honest and reliable workers. Young Dutch-American women received frequent offers to work as household help because of their neatness and good manners; Dutch boys were valued as farmhands for many of the same reasons. The Dutch won acceptance easily in Protestant America, in part because their Calvinist creed mirrored many beliefs of the English Puritans who laid the groundwork of American culture. And although they were often teased about their foreign

*In 1910 schoolchildren play in Holland, Michigan.*

*A portrait of Dominie Henrik Scholte.*

speech or Old World style of dress (women wore their hair up in white scarves and donned wooden shoes), the Dutch never had to withstand the persecution endured by many other ethnic groups. In fact, Dutch enclaves such as the one established in Holland were admired by many Americans as model immigrant communities.

## The Dutch Across America

Although Holland, Michigan, was one of the earliest and most successful of the 19th-century Dutch settlements, it was not the only one. Some Dutch immigrants put down roots in New York, because the vast majority of immigrants from the Netherlands disembarked there after the overseas journey. As did their 17th-century forebears, many Dutch of the 19th century founded farming villages north of Manhattan. These smaller communities often contained Dutch from the same home province: For example, those from Zeeland settled in Sayville, New York; whereas immigrants from the Frisian Islands, located just off the coast of the Netherlands, made their home in the New York town of Lancaster.

Most Dutch arrivals, however, pushed into the nation's interior rather than remain on the East Coast, many following their ministers to frontier terrain within the United States. In 1847 a dominie named Hendrik Scholte led 800 emigrants from the Netherlands to settle on 18,000 acres of Iowa farmland purchased from the U.S. government. The Scholte contingent named its new community Pella, in honor of a town in the New Testament that served as a refuge for persecuted Christians.

The Pella settlers had few problems in comparison to their countrymen in Holland, Michigan. Early arrivals in Pella built sod houses out of the soft, moist land they would farm, cutting the dirt into large slabs, erecting walls and a roof, and covering the outside with grasses. The farming of prairie proved easier than the cultivation of wilderness. The Iowans were aided, too, by a relatively mild climate. Nevertheless, they strug-

*In 1855 Scholte's congregants built this church in Pella, Iowa. The Latin inscription on the front of the building reads: "In God is our hope and refuge."*

gled with crop failures, droughts, grasshopper plagues, dust storms, prairie fires, and dry electrical storms that sent balls of blue flame rolling across the farm belt and Plains. Sudden and serious blizzards could blow for three days straight, reducing visibility dramatically. Those unfortunate enough to get caught in such storms would sometimes die in their own backyards, not knowing how to find their houses in the whirling snow. Despite all these obstacles, the Dutch of Iowa prospered, and their children created Dutch communities in adjoining states as land around Pella became increasingly expensive.

Still other Dutch-American communities sprang up under the direction of Dutch Catholics who emigrated to escape religious repression in the Protestant homeland. In 1848 Father Theodorus Van den Broek led approximately 350 immigrants to Fox River, Wisconsin, which became one of several Dutch Catholic communities in northern Wisconsin. Unlike their Protestant countrymen, Dutch Catholics received no financial support or aid from existing congregations, which were all Protestant. Despite their poverty, the settlement survived and even drew more Catholics from the Netherlands to Wisconsin.

In 1850 a Dutch-Catholic immigrant named Arnold Verstegen and his family arrived in Little Chute, Wisconsin, a town located near Fox River. At first Verstegen lamented his decision to come to America, but within a few months he was enjoying his new life immensely, and his long correspondence with his father-in-law in North Brabant, Holland, captured the enthusiasm felt by many within the Dutch community. In 1852 Verstegen wrote:

> We have more and better food than we ever had in Holland; we live in a warm house and have good clothes; we have Mass in our church each Sunday; and the children go to school and catechism. . . . Now, Father, you will understand why we love our new country, and you will not be surprised when I say that we have made up our minds to make it our home for the rest of our days, bringing up our children to become American citizens.

Twenty years after his move to America, Arnold Verstegen was a happy and prosperous man: "When I first came here I felt as if I was fated to lead the life of a hermit the rest of my living days, and now I am surrounded by more luxuries than I have ever seen." For some immigrants, America may indeed have lived up to all expectations.

## The Dutch Contribution

As the Midwest attracted increasing numbers of Dutch and other immigrants from northern Europe, new settlers ranged farther west to find cheap farmland. Many profited by the Homestead Act of 1862, federal legislation that granted willing pioneers 160 acres each of public land for only a nominal fee and the promise that they would clear and settle the land. By 1900 the approximately 250,000 Dutch who had migrated to the United States during the 19th century had established communities in nearly every state, especially in the northern half of the country.

Although 250,000 seems a huge migration, emigrants from the Netherlands composed only one-hundredth of the 25 million newcomers who arrived in the United States during the second half of the 19th century alone. Still, the Dutch contribution to the development of the United States is among the most significant of any ethnic group: They helped open the West to settlement; drained the marshes around Chicago and created small farms in the land around the city; cleared the forests of western Michigan; built harbors, small businesses, and successful towns; broke the prairie sod of the Plains; grew grains; and bred livestock. In this way the Dutch found their own niche in the booming and bustling world of 19th-century America.

But toward the end of the century, growing cities spread into outlying rural areas, and many Dutch communities were absorbed into new suburbs. Their new proximity to mainstream U.S. society speeded their assimilation into American life. Thus the Dutch-American farming community yielded to suburban American society.

Like other immigrant groups, the Dutch were ambivalent about becoming Americans. They were usually eager for citizenship; a county clerk who visited Holland, Michigan, one year after its founding received 300 applications for citizenship from the Dutch who lived there. Like Arnold Verstegen they were proud of raising their children to be Americans. But they also clung to important parts of their ethnic identity—their religion, their language, and most important, their relationships with their countrymen.

Martin Van Buren, the eighth president of the United States, claims in his autobiography that his eldest son was the first in six generations of his family in

America to marry someone who was not Dutch. Marriage within the Dutch community, which kept families from losing their ethnic identity, was common both among prominent New York Dutch families and within the close pioneer Dutch communities of the Midwest.

But eventually a majority of Dutch children chose to move away from their parents' communities to find work in large cities. As memories of the Netherlands died with each passing generation, young Dutch Americans began to think of themselves as Americans first. For the Dutch this process began early in American history because they arrived at the beginning of colonization and found they had much in common with the region's British settlers.

In the 20th century there were new pressures toward Americanization. During World War I nationalism grew, and Americans, confusing the Dutch with the Germans, became antagonistic toward Dutch efforts to maintain their old customs. They interpreted cultural separateness as a lack of patriotism and were suspicious of people who did not speak English. During this time politicians passed laws requiring the use of English, and

*(continued on page 73)*

*In about 1900 a Dutch farm family stands before a wagon loaded with produce for the Chicago market.*

# VISTAS AND VISIONS

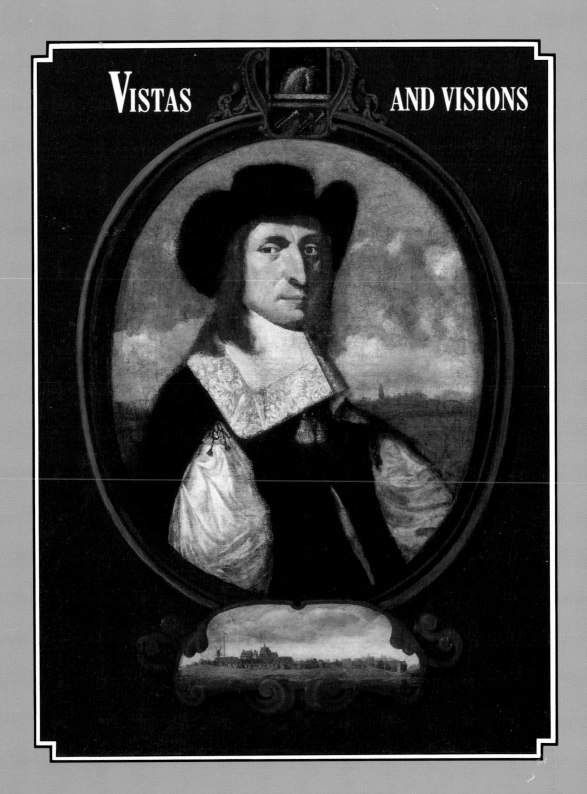

Dutch Americans can boast a long history of political achievement. Cornelis Steenwyck (overleaf), a civic leader in New Amsterdam, became mayor in 1668, four years after the British takeover. Philip Schuyler (below), with his family in their Schuylerville, N.Y., home, served as a member of the New York State legislature. Dutch Americans attained economic as well as political success, as shown in oil portraits of Pau De Wanderdaer (opposite) and Mary Beekman (right), Dutch colonists from prominent families.

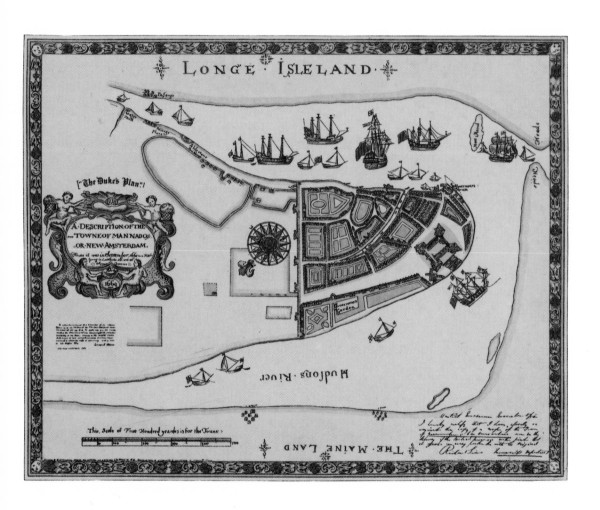

*Illustrations of New Amsterdam grace two maps of the region: Ships anchor off Manhattan Island in a view of the settlement ca. 1664 (above); a panorama of the Lower Hudson is spotlighted in a map of the Atlantic coastline dating from about 1700 (above, right). In an 18th-century engraving (below, right) a seated figure representing New Amsterdam yields a beaver pelt to a standing "New York," symbol of the new regime.*

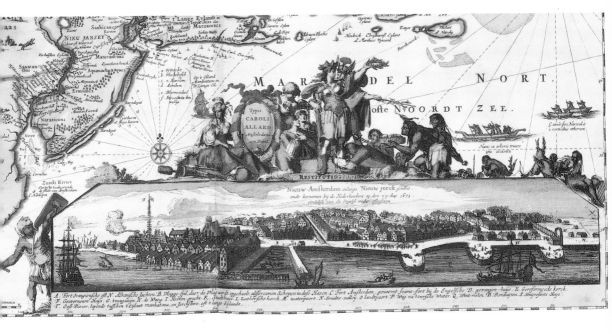

*Landscape paintings capture the beauty of New Netherland's terrain. Here two works depict Dutch-founded communities along the Hudson: one, a small riverside village; the other, Poughkeepsie, New York, a bustling industrial town (below).*

*A painting created in 1846 by William Hart portrays Albany, a Dutch-founded town that is now New York's state capital.*

Sunny Morning on the Hudson *by Thomas Cole (1801–48), America's first important landscape painter and founder of an artistic movement known as the Hudson River school. Cole's paintings capture the idyllic natural beauty of upper New York State—a region first settled by Dutch colonists.*

(continued from page 64)
soon afterward the government instituted new quotas that limited immigration. Thus the Dutch, like other immigrants, received an extra push to become Americans.

For better or worse the Dutch slipped gradually and easily into American society. By the first decades of the 20th century, the unique culture of the Dutch had largely died out in the United States. The grandchildren of midwestern Dutch settlers were indistinguishable in speech, customs, and dress from the offspring of a dozen immigrant groups from Europe or the British Isles. Even the influx of 80,000 Dutch who came to America after the devastation of Nazi occupation during World War II was not enough to revitalize Dutch culture in the country.

In one sense, though, the rapid assimilation of the Dutch in the United States benefited these people. Americans of long standing welcomed them warmly into fields closed to other immigrants, such as business or politics. And descendants of the Dutch found themselves in the center of American affairs, with access to persons of power and—as in the case of three U.S. presidents—entry into some of the highest offices in the land. ✒

*In the early 1900s some Dutch-American inhabitants of Zeeland, Michigan, drove traditional hay wagons, but others drove automobiles.*

*In 1907 President Theodore Roosevelt addresses a rally in Indianapolis, Indiana.*

# THE DUTCH IN AMERICAN POLITICS

Seldom popular, heroic, or brilliant, [the Dutch] provided experienced day-to-day leadership, overcoming small crises, marshalling limited resources, hanging on beyond hope or expectation until circumstances turned in their favor. Thus, Schuyler's army was at hand and ready to fight for liberty at Saratoga under Gates and Arnold; Van Buren's party was at hand and ready to sweep democracy into the White House under Andrew Jackson; Franklin Roosevelt's organization was at hand and ready to support the world struggle for freedom as defined by Winston Churchill.

—*The Gansevoorts of Albany* by Alice P. Kenney

**D**utch Americans have left their stamp on American politics. Although their influence has not been as evident as that of other ethnic groups, most notably the Irish, Dutch Americans can lay claim to a long and proud history of statesmanship. By 1664, when New Amsterdam fell to a British invasion and was rechristened New York, a few prominent Dutch families wielded most of the power within the colony. These powerful clans—leaders in commerce, society, and civic life—governed in the interests of all.

Most of these "knickerbocker" families—so called after Diedrich Knickerbocker, a fictional Dutchman created by Washington Irving—had amassed their fortune in one of three fields: agriculture, commerce, or industry. Together such families as the Van Cortlandts, the Van Rensselaers, the Beekans, the Banckers, the Rutgers, the Van Hornes, the Philipses (who owned nearly 1 million acres along the Hudson River), the Schuylers, the Van Dams, the Stuyvesants, and the Roosevelts controlled most of the property and held many of the public offices in New York State.

## The Gansevoorts

Perhaps the Gansevoort family—one of the most prominent New York clans—best typifies the Dutch-American rise to power. In 1660 Harmen Harmense van Gansevoort arrived in New Netherland and made his way to Beverwyck, a Dutch settlement just south of what is now Albany, New York, and a center of the colony's fur trade.

Van Gansevoort moved from business to business, acquiring small enterprises cheaply, building them up, and selling them at a profit. He established a brewery with his earnings from these ventures and thus supported his family with a steady source of income.

After Harmen's death, his son Leendert guided the growth of the modest brewery, expanding it into a thriving company that provided the basis for a family fortune. Wealthy and ambitious, Leendert aspired to enter the upper crust of Dutch society. He left the Lutheran religion in order to join the Dutch Reformed church alongside other important Hudson Valley families. He also became a landowner and won a post as a local official in 1734. Despite such tangible evidence of success, Leendert van Gansevoort was excluded from the most privileged circle of New Netherland families—all fur traders who regarded "new merchants" like him with contempt.

*Father Knickerbocker—a creation of writer Washington Irving— was a favorite subject of American cartoonists.*

True acceptance eluded the van Gansevoorts until the third generation of the family—Leendert's sons Johannes, Pieter, and Harme—reached adulthood. The three brothers entered different professions; Johannes maintained the family brewery, Pieter practiced medicine, and Harme opened his own store in 1739. All three commanded the respect of their community and won appointment to city offices in Albany. Harme, in particular, achieved social as well as political success by marrying into a rich Dutch family from Kinderhook, New York. By the time of his death he had become one of the wealthiest and most revered men in Albany. His rise to eminence paralleled the coming of age of the Dutch merchant class (as opposed to the old aristocracy of fur traders) in New Netherland. Indeed, the Gansevoorts remained a leading Albany family for six generations.

*In about 1730 Leendert and Catarina van Gansevoort sit for their oil portraits.*

## Dutch in the War of Independence

During the revolutionary war, many young scions of prominent Dutch families earned a place in American politics not by winning an official post but by taking up arms in the patriot cause. Harme van Gansevoort's son Peter fought for George Washington's army and attained the rank of general, along with two other descendants of Dutch colonial families, Philip Schuyler and Abraham Broeck. In 1775 Peter accompanied Washington's forces to Canada in order to prevent the British army from using America's northern neighbor as a base for attacks against the 13 colonies. When the Canadian campaign failed in its purpose, Peter retreated

*During the American War of Independence, Colonel Peter Gansevoort carried this flag, unique to his regiment, the Third New York Continentals.*

EXCELSIOR

with the patriot army to upstate New York, where he helped to defend Fort Stanwix—a crucial strategic holding—against the British during the summer of 1776.

Philip Van Cortlandt was another Dutch New Yorker who rose in the ranks of the American revolutionary army. In October 1781 he fought in the decisive battle of Yorktown, in which the combined American and French forces shattered the last of the British army. In his memoirs, written many years after the event, he recalls the first shot fired at Yorktown:

> I could hear the [cannon] Ball strike from House to house, and I was afterwards Informed that it went thro the one where many officers were at dinner and over the Tables discomposing the Dishes, and [the cannon ball] Either Killed or wounded the one at the head of the Table and I also heard that gun was fired by the Commr. in Chief [George Washington] who was designedly present in the battery for the express purpose of putting the first match.

The Schuylers, the Van Cortlandts, and the Gansevoorts were among many prominent Dutch families who sent their sons to fight for American independence, yet they represented only a fraction of the New York Dutch community, which was divided in its allegiances. Whereas Albany families tended to support the American cause, the Dutch in the southern half of the state, which was occupied by the British for most of the war, tended to side with the redcoats. Wealthy Dutch colonists, still residing in what had once been New Amsterdam, combined forces with the region's sizable population of aristocratic British families in order to protect interests common to both groups.

Most Dutch in southern New York—rich or not—expressed skepticism about the ability of patriot leaders to govern a growing country. The great majority of Dutch colonists earned their living as traders or merchants and feared the loss of British customers for their goods and the end of British protection for their com-

*In this 19th-century engraving a female member of the Schuyler family sets her wheat fields afire rather than yield them to advancing British troops.*

merce. Just as the European Dutch frequently refused to take sides in international conflicts, so the average Dutch American preferred neutrality and hoped not to confront either side but to avoid any decisive action that might result in financial ruin. Their most lasting achievement in the historic conflict mirrored their peacetime accomplishments: Several powerful Dutch merchants helped finance the patriots' struggle.

## A New Era

At war's end, Dutch Americans returned to the well-ordered lives they had known before the tumultuous 1770s. No public event mobilized them until the 1840s. During that decade the farmers of the Hudson Valley organized against big landowners who still retained a great many of their 200-year-old privileges from the patroonships established by the Dutch West India Company. These landholders squeezed independent farmers of their profits by demanding unreasonably high taxes of them. From 1839 to 1846 the small farmers of the Hudson Valley—many of them Dutch—rebelled against these taxes. After seven years of agitation, the landowners agreed to renegotiate the leases for the farms and granted their tenants fair and favorable terms.

Dutch farmers of this era faced an even more serious conflict, one concerning the issue of slavery. As farmers, many had relied on slave labor and had opposed the state abolition of slavery in 1799. In the early 19th century, a nationwide movement to abolish slavery, known as abolitionism, gained thousands of followers throughout the North. Most Dutch concerned themselves with the pragmatic rather than the moral implications of the debate over slavery—a conflict that ultimately led to the outbreak of the American Civil War in 1861.

Before 1860, the Dutch had cast their ballots with the Democratic party, which had traditionally welcomed immigrants of varying ethnicities into its ranks. But as Lincoln's antislavery Republican party gained a following, many Dutch shifted their loyalty to the Republicans, in part drawn by the party's liberal home-

*A lithograph depicts a critical moment in "anti-rent wars" waged between landowners and small farmers in the Hudson Valley. In 1839 the Albany County Militia (pictured at right) was sent into the valley to quell the protest.*

steading legislation. During the Civil War, Dutch Americans, like other Northerners, vowed to preserve the Union and thus sided with the antislavery forces.

## The First Dutch-American President

By the latter half of the 19th century, Dutch Americans had split into two factions. The monied New York Dutch formed one branch of the community, the new arrivals in the Midwest another. Both groups held conservative political views but for vastly different reasons. Those from wealthy New York families fought against any change that might threaten their long-standing affluence and power; newly arrived Dutch shied away from innovative political ideas that seemed to challenge their strong Calvinist beliefs and traditional ethics.

But established Dutch Americans and newcomers alike took great pride in the election of a fellow kinsman, Martin Van Buren, to the presidency. Born in 1782, Van Buren—the son of a tavern keeper—grew to adulthood in the Hudson Valley town Kinderhook, New York. A lawyer by profession, he immersed himself in Democratic party politics as a young man, serving as a U.S. senator from 1821 to 1828 and as governor of New York from 1828 to 1829. He resigned his office to act as secretary of state to Andrew Jackson during his presidency. From 1832 to 1836 Van Buren served as Jackson's vice-president, then in 1836 was elected president.

During Van Buren's four years in the White House, the United States suffered an economic depression that spurred the collapse of prominent banking houses and led to rioting in New York over inflated food prices. In answer to this crisis, Van Buren reformed the nation's treasury system. He also fought for states' right to govern themselves with minimal interference from the federal government. Van Buren ran for reelection in 1840 but lacked public support, mainly because of the economic crisis that had plagued the country during his administration, and lost to William Henry Harrison. He died in 1862, the second year of the Civil War.

Van Buren was the first Dutch American to hold the nation's highest office, but he was not the only one. Theodore Roosevelt and his distant cousin Franklin Delano Roosevelt, both descendants of one of the most distinguished Dutch-American families in the United States, are remembered as two of the most beloved American presidents of the 20th century.

## Theodore Roosevelt

Theodore and Franklin Delano Roosevelt both traced their lineage back to Klaes Martensen van Roosevelt, who arrived in America in 1644. After purchasing a tract of land in what is now the Murray Hill neighbor-

*Theodore Roosevelt donned a buckskin ensemble for this portrait in 1885.*

hood of New York City, Klaes van Roosevelt tried his hand at agriculture and built up a successful small farm. He passed it on to his eldest son, Nicholas, who declined to enter the family business. Instead, he sold the farm and moved upstate, where he established himself as a fur trader. After several years he had saved a small fortune and returned to New Amsterdam, where his successful business ventures swelled the family coffers. As the van Roosevelts accumulated wealth, they also secured their high social standing through marriages to other prominent Dutch colonial families. They remained at the top of New York society for more than 200 years. By 1858, when Theodore was born, the van Roosevelts had become simply the Roosevelts.

Theodore Roosevelt, known to family and nation alike as Teddy, entered the world on East 20th Street in New York City, not far from the site of Klaes van Roosevelt's Murray Hill farm. Roosevelt began his childhood as a sickly boy but offset his weakness by pursuing a course of rigorous physical activity that included weight lifting, boxing, rowing, and swimming in order to counteract a naturally frail constitution. He had an equal appreciation for intellectual challenges. He graduated from Harvard University in 1880 and enrolled in the law school at Columbia University. During that year he wed Alice Hathaway Lee, a Boston socialite, who bore him a daughter, also named Alice.

In 1882 Roosevelt won a seat as a Republican state legislator, but when his term ended in 1884 he left politics in the face of personal tragedy: Just four years after his marriage, his wife suffered an untimely death and his mother died, a victim of typhoid fever. In his grief he retreated to the Dakota Bad Lands to live as a cattle rancher, but the lure of politics drew him back to public life by 1886, when he ran as the Republican candidate for mayor of New York City. He lost the election but remained involved with city affairs, first acting as Civil Service commissioner, then becoming president of the New York City Board of Police Commissioners. In 1897 Roosevelt broke into national politics when President William McKinley appointed him to a cabinet post, assistant secretary of the navy. In his new position, Roosevelt drew on the naval knowledge he had gained more than a decade earlier when he wrote *Naval History of the War of 1812*. That volume was only one of several he penned, including *Hunting Trips of a Ranchman*, *The Winning of the West*, and *Through the Brazilian Wilderness*.

The very year after his appointment to the Department of the Navy, however, Roosevelt again abandoned the life of a public servant for more rugged pursuits. In 1898 he volunteered for military duty in the Spanish-American War, in which the United States supported nearby Cuba in a war of independence against Spain. Roosevelt's regiment, the First Volunteer Cavalry Regiment, was known informally as the Rough Riders because its members took great pride in their fortitude and bravery. On July 1, 1898, Roosevelt achieved his supreme moment of glory in the Battle of San Juan Hill, in which he distinguished himself. At war's end, Roosevelt returned home from Cuba a war hero and won the Republican nomination for the 1898 gubernatorial election in New York State.

In 1899 Theodore Roosevelt was again chosen for a national appointment, this time as the vice-president of William McKinley during the latter's second term as

*Theodore Roosevelt and the Rough Riders pose atop the hill they captured during the Battle of San Juan.*

president. Roosevelt expressed grave reservations about entering what he saw as a ceremonial office, one lacking either importance or power. But in the end he agreed to join McKinley's reelection campaign in the hope that a tenure as vice-president would strengthen his chances of winning the presidency for himself in 1904.

Roosevelt wait lasted not four years but six months. In September 1901—just half a year after the victorious McKinley-Roosevelt ticket was sworn into office— McKinley fell to the bullet of an assassin, thus forcing Theodore Roosevelt to assume the responsibilities of the nation's chief executive. At 41 he became the youngest president in American history. During his eight years in office (he won reelection in 1904), Roosevelt had many accomplishments. One of his major coups was protecting the natural beauty of the United States. He championed the cause of conservation, adding 230 million acres to land owned by the U.S. government and protected from unregulated development. He doubled the number of national parks, created the country's 50 wildlife refuges, and established 18 national monuments.

Just as Roosevelt fought to preserve American wilderness against the encroachment of man, so he also sought to shield American business from the domination of large corporations. He supported trust-busting measures that prevented American companies from holding monopolies on essential goods and services. Roosevelt was equally influential in foreign affairs: He sponsored the Panama Canal, promoted an aggressive foreign policy in Latin America, and in 1906 negotiated the end of a war between Russia and Japan. The next year he was awarded the Nobel Peace Prize for his efforts.

A charismatic and opinionated man, Roosevelt charmed voters but alienated the conservative wing of his own party. By the end of his elected term, he was so disillusioned with his fellow Republicans that he declined to seek reelection in 1908. In 1912, after losing the Republican nomination, he ran as the Progressive party candidate for the presidency. Despite his great personal popularity, Roosevelt lost to Democrat Woodrow Wilson. He then retired to his family retreat, Sagamore Hill, located in Oyster Bay, New York. He died there in 1919.

## The Second President Roosevelt

Accomplished as Theodore Roosevelt was, he was outshone as president by his younger cousin, Franklin Delano Roosevelt, who guided the nation back to prosperity after the economic collapse of the Great Depression and then proved an outstanding commander in chief during World War II. Franklin Roosevelt was born in 1882 in Hyde Park, New York, the son of a patrician family. He attended the prestigious Groton School, Harvard University, and Columbia University Law School but never distinguished himself as an outstanding student. While at Columbia he married his distant cousin Eleanor Roosevelt, who later rose to international prominence in her own right.

In 1910 Roosevelt entered politics as the Democratic nominee for the New York State Senate. Although he was a dark horse candidate for the seat, Roosevelt threw

*In 1889 seven-year-old Franklin Delano Roosevelt (second from left) poses for a portrait with his mother's family on the Delanos' New York estate, Algonac.*

*Franklin Roosevelt during his tenure as assistant secretary of the navy.*

himself into campaigning and, with Eleanor often at his side, made as many as 10 speeches a day. He traveled most often to the small farming communities that clustered along the Hudson River—the region where his Dutch ancestors had won their first great successes in America. Roosevelt's natural warmth and easy manner won him many new supporters, who swept him into office in an upset victory.

Like his cousin Theodore, whom he idolized, Franklin Roosevelt took an interest in conservation, and he, too, entered national politics. In 1913 President Wilson appointed him assistant secretary of the navy. In Washington, D.C., Roosevelt won a reputation for efficiency and leadership, and at the Democratic convention of 1920 he was nominated to be the running partner of James M. Cox, the presidential nominee.

Although the Democrats lost the election in a Republican landslide, Roosevelt maintained his optimism about his own career, telling a friend, "The moment of defeat is the best time to lay plans for future victories."

Roosevelt suffered a grave setback in 1919 when he was stricken with polio, a disease of the muscles that permanently paralyzed his legs. Although he was in enormous physical pain, he refused to retreat into invalidism. He made frequent visits to a spa at Warm Springs, Georgia, where he underwent a regimen of hydrotherapy; furthermore, he resolved never to appear helpless, dependent, or defeated by the disease.

By the late 1920s Roosevelt was back on the political track. He staged a triumphant return by speaking at the Democratic National Convention of 1924, then he yielded to party pressure to run for governor of New York and won the gubernatorial election of 1928. From his seat in Albany, New York's state capital, Roosevelt watched the nation's economy fall to ruin under the administration of President Herbert Hoover, a Republican. In October 1929 the stock market crashed and investors endured unprecedented losses amounting to approximately $50 billion. Even worse, unemployment took its toll on nearly 12 million Americans, and the threat of widespread social unrest loomed closer. These dire conditions set the stage for a Democratic victory in the next election.

The party chose Roosevelt as their candidate in the election of 1932, and he delivered them a sweeping victory. Once in office, he assembled a group of expert advisers, dubbed the brain trust, who advised him to institute a program of radical reform. Roosevelt thus enacted a series of acts—known collectively as the New Deal—that are widely credited with forestalling economic collapse. More important, Roosevelt's New Deal agencies (the Federal Emergency Relief Administration, the National Recovery Administration, the Public Works Administration, and the Works Progress Administration, among others) relieved the hunger of millions of starving Americans by providing them with

food, money, or jobs. The nation's economic recovery was speeded by the onset of World War II, which America entered in 1941. The booming defense industries equipped the Allies with weapons and bolstered the American economy by hiring millions of workers. In wartime as well as peacetime Roosevelt proved an accomplished statesman who projected calm and self-confidence even during such disasters as the Japanese bombing of the American fleet at Pearl Harbor. America's Roosevelt, England's prime minister Winston Churchill, and Russia's premier Josef Stalin—known as the Big Three—together deflected the menace of Nazism.

But Roosevelt, in his fourth term of office by 1945, did not live to see the conclusion of war either in Europe or in the Pacific arena. On April 12, 1945, he suffered a massive cerebral hemorrhage and died at his traditional retreat, Warm Springs, Georgia. When the president's funeral cortege walked through the streets of Washington, D.C., onlookers thronged the streets and the nation mourned one of the greatest leaders in the history of the American presidency. ∾

*In 1944 President Roosevelt sits between Soviet premier Josef Stalin and British prime minister Winston Churchill during a conference of the Big Three Allied powers at Teheran, Iran.*

*In 1985 Bruce Springsteen*
*performs during a concert tour*
*launched to promote his album*
Born in the USA.

# DUTCH AMERICANS
# OF ACHIEVEMENT

Dutch Americans have often been praised for their talents at politics and business, but their gifts extend far beyond the world of commerce into such varied fields as film, sports, music, and engineering. Most Americans have no idea they are enjoying the fruits of Dutch-American creativity when they watch a classic Hollywood epic directed by Cecil B. DeMille, puzzle over a painting by Willem de Kooning, listen to a hit record by rock-and-roll master Bruce Springsteen, or drive a car produced by the Chrysler Corporation, a company founded by a Dutch American.

## A Great American Engineer

Born in 1875, Walter Percy Chrysler was descended from Tuenis Van Dolsen, an early inhabitant of New Amsterdam. Chrysler grew up far from the elite society of East Coast Dutch America, in Wamego, Kansas. As a young man he impressed his teachers with his intelligence, but he eschewed a formal college education in order to accept an apprenticeship in the machine shops of the Union Pacific Railroad. There he learned his craft and developed into a first-rate machinist.

*A young Walter Chrysler sits for the camera in about 1885.*

The Union Pacific offered Chrysler a lifetime of economic stability—a steady job at good wages—but he had no desire to settle there and instead set out for the West, where he plied his trade for a succession of railroad companies, all enjoying an industry-wide boom. Chrysler changed jobs frequently and earned a reputation as a crackerjack mechanic first in Salt Lake City, later with the Chicago Great Western Company, and finally with the American Locomotive Company in Pittsburgh, Pennsylvania.

Just as he entered company management, Chrysler again changed direction and accepted a drastic pay cut in order to pursue a new interest in the budding automobile industry. In 1912 he accepted a job as works manager for the Buick Motor Company, then a division of General Motors, in Detroit. Drawing on his technical expertise, Chrysler revolutionized Buick's method of production by reorganizing the factory assembly line. In 1916, only four years after his arrival, he was named president of Buick. He held this position for another four years, making a name for himself as a manager who could reverse the fortunes of an ailing car company through innovating its method of production.

In 1921 Chrysler was hired to work for the Willys-Overland Company, one of the major automobile manufacturers of its day, and was charged with overhauling the declining firm. He succeeded in his task and was soon wooed away from Willys-Overland by one of its competitors, the Maxwell Motor Company. Chrysler soon assumed the presidency of Maxwell and introduced a new line of automobile, the Chrysler car, to the company assembly line. The Chrysler offered the American consumers such technologically advanced features as four-wheel hydraulic brakes and a high-compression engine. The new automobile met with such success that within one year the Maxwell Motor Company had become the Chrysler Corporation.

In 1928 Walter Chrysler expanded his outfit by merging it with the Dodge Brothers Company, another automaker, and within seven years his grew into one of the largest automobile manufacturers in the country, second only to that of Henry Ford. In 1935 the one-time mechanic retired from the presidency of Chrysler to become its chairman. By that time he not only merited a chapter in the annals of American industry but also secured a place in the history of the nation's architecture. New York City's Chrysler Building, completed in 1929, ranked then as the tallest building in the world and still stands as an eloquent monument to the jazz-age design of the 1920s. Walter Chrysler died at his New York estate in 1940, three years after completing his autobiography, *Life of an American Workman.*

## A Hollywood Legend

During the time that Chrysler innovated car design, his contemporary Cecil Blount DeMille revolutionized motion pictures. During his four decades in Hollywood, DeMille produced and directed 66 screenplays. His movies, according to critic Robert Sklar, "provided a voyeuristic glimpse of forbidden pleasures and desires."

DeMille was born in 1881 in Ashfield, Massachusetts, and learned the thespian's art at an early age through exposure to the stage productions of his father, an actor. For a time DeMille followed in his footsteps and tried his hand at stage acting, but he quickly discovered that a career in the theater would condemn him to a life of poverty. He chose instead to gamble his future on a new entertainment industry, motion pictures.

In 1913 he launched his movie career in New York City by filming stage hits such as *The Squaw Man*, which he made in New York in partnership with Samuel Goldwyn, who later became one of Hollywood's most renowned movie moguls. Encouraged by his modest success with his New York productions, DeMille set out for California, the new center for the motion picture industry. He improvised his first office in a barn, sharing the space with a cow and a horse, but he thrived despite his meager surroundings.

*A middle-aged Walter Chrysler poses for a photograph on the deck of a cruise ship.*

*Cecil B. DeMille confers with actors Claudette Colbert and Fredric March on the set of* The Sign of the Cross.

Within a year DeMille had mastered the technical side of film production and innovated the practice of filming in sunshine rather than in artificial light. He also possessed other talents ideal to filmmaking. He had an instinctive and accurate sense of popular taste, and he displayed a gift for seeing which actors—all of whom had learned their art on stage—could translate their talents to the silent screen. Movie legends such as Gloria Swanson appeared in DeMille's films early in their careers.

In 1919 DeMille created a scandal by casting Swanson in *Male and Female* and filming her virtually naked, stepping into a sunken bathtub. The movie provoked public outrage and became a box office success, helping to establish its director as a major force in Hollywood. In 1924, on the strength of his early accomplishments, he formed the Cecil DeMille Pictures Corporation. There he created his trademark works: movies based on biblical themes. *The Ten Commandments* (1923) and *King of Kings* (1927) called for casts of hundreds—costumed in exotic garments—who paraded before sets spectacular in their ornate detail. As historian Robert Sklar writes in *Movie-Made America*: DeMille "discovered the most congenial form for his particular skills, the religious epic, which proved the perfect vehicle for his deft combination of moral didacticism and orgiastic fantasy.''

In 1928 DeMille joined Metro-Goldwyn-Mayer at the invitation of his old friend Samuel Goldwyn. His career continued to flourish as the studios switched from silent films to talkies. In 1932 he directed his first talking picture, *The Sign of the Cross*, for Paramount. He easily adapted his work to the next great innovation in the industry, Technicolor, which was in wide use during the 1940s. Although he remained active until his death in 1959, DeMille never surpassed his classic early work, movies that have made his name synonymous with the heyday of Hollywood glamour.

## Willem de Kooning

As Cecil DeMille's lavish films introduced a new opulence to American motion pictures, the complex works of Dutch-American painter Willem de Kooning brought a renewed dynamism to the nation's fine arts. Born in the Netherlands in 1904, de Kooning displayed an early talent for drawing and enrolled at the Rotterdam Academy of Fine Arts and Techniques at about age 16. There he excelled at classical techniques of draftsmanship, mastering the difficult skills of foreshortening, modeling, and rendering light and shadow. In 1926, after several years of commercial art experience, he came to America hoping to find work as an illustrator. He soon abandoned this effort, however, recalling later, ''I had no talent for it.''

De Kooning spent the next few years in New York, supporting himself at odd jobs such as house painting and sign making and devoting his free time to painting and drawing in his studio on West 44th Street in Manhattan. In 1935 he joined the Federal Arts Project, a division of the Works Progress Administration, a government organization established to aid fine artists during the years of the Great Depression by providing them with work and a small income. Along with other New Deal artists, de Kooning planned murals to be painted on public buildings.

*Willem de Kooning in his studio.*

In the 1930s de Kooning still worked at realistic renderings of natural or everyday objects, such as an arrangement of ceramic bowls, but in 1931 he met a fellow artist, Arshile Gorky, under whose influence he began to move away from faithfully depicting external reality in his work. One of his earliest patrons, poet and dance critic Edwin Denby, later recollected an incident from this period in the artist's life: "I met Willem de Kooning on the fire escape because a black kitten lost in the rain cried at my fire door. And after the rain it turned out to be his kitten. He was painting a dark, eight-foot picture that had sweeps of black across it and a big look. That was early in 1936."

During the 1940s de Kooning and several other artists, including painters Hans Hofmann and Robert Motherwell, formed the vanguard of a uniquely American artistic movement known as abstract expressionism. This bold style transformed reality into complex visual statements abounding with geometric shapes, sweeping lines, and planes of color. In 1948 de Kooning unveiled his paintings at a one-man exhibition that established him as one of the leading figures in the American art world. His complicated canvases puzzled and often outraged viewers accustomed to conventional modes of artistic expression.

In fact, de Kooning never completely abandoned his old method of working. Just two years after his landmark 1948 show he began work on the painting *Woman I*, which seemed to bridge both representational and abstract styles. According to the art critic Harold Rosenberg, one of the early voices to champion de Kooning:

> [T]he thing that de Kooning did was to discover that for a painter like himself, who had been painting for already 20 or more years, the figure would emerge spontaneously out of the act of painting. Obviously, you have certain habits, and if you really let yourself go, you would not produce a mess, you'd produce a figure.

*In 1955 Willem de Kooning painted* Composition, *a work rendered in the abstract expressionist style.*

Alternately regarded as suggestive or grotesque, de Kooning's series of *Woman* paintings brought further acclaim to his career— still a productive one in the late 1980s.

## The Future of Rock and Roll

Willem de Kooning has won international acclaim for his talent, yet his work does not reach the broad audience enjoyed by popular performers such as rock-and-roller Bruce Springsteen. Springsteen—perhaps the most adored musical figure of the late 1970s and 1980s—was born to an Italian-American mother and Dutch-American father in 1949. Raised in the New Jersey town of Freehold, he developed an early sympathy with the thousands of Americans, just like him, living

*In 1984 Bruce Springsteen jams with E Street Band saxophonist Clarence Clemons in Oakland, California.*

in working-class towns across the country. Springsteen's father drifted from job to job; his mother worked as a secretary. The lyrics to his songs describe the desolation he experienced as a young man, trapped in a blue-collar ghetto.

Springsteen credits music with his own escape from Freehold. In 1975 he told a *Time* magazine interviewer, "From the beginning my guitar was something I could go to. If I hadn't found music, I don't know what I would have done." By age 14 Springsteen had learned the rudiments of playing the guitar, harmonica, and piano. He found a welcome in local pick-up bands and spent every spare moment of his life playing and writing music. "Music was my way of keeping people from looking through and around me. I wanted the heavies to know I was around," he later admitted. Soon he began forming his own bands, groups with names such as the Rogues, the Castiles, the Steel Mill, and Dr. Zoom and the Sonic Boom.

Springsteen played regular gigs throughout this era but found a following only in the New Jersey clubs where he had gotten his start. He remained unknown until 1972, when a young rock producer named Mike Appel arranged an audition for Springsteen with John Hammond, the vice-president of talent acquisition at Columbia Records. Hammond later told *Newsweek* about his first encounter with Springsteen: "The kid absolutely knocked me out. You only hear somebody really good once every ten years, and not only was Bruce the best, he was a lot better than Dylan when I first heard him."

Indeed, Columbia Records drew many comparisons between Dylan and Springsteen in publicizing the latter's first album, *Greetings from Asbury Park,* released in 1973. Although praised by critics, the album was allotted little air time by most radio stations and sold slowly. Springsteen continued undiscouraged, performing live with his E Street Band for a growing circle of admirers who cheered his renditions of rock classics as well as his own songs. Word of Springsteen's hard-edged rock compositions spread to popular music critics across the country, who began to pay attention to the singer from New Jersey.

In 1973 Bruce Pollock wrote in the *New York Times*: "Springsteen is a word virtuoso. His lyrics are intuitive, emotional, a mass of flung images that spin toward you from all directions and somehow hang on a canvas— great swatches of local color that blend into a landscape of remembered adolescent scenes and dreams." But one review, in particular, focused a spotlight on Springsteen and subsequently thrust him into national prominence. In Boston's *Real Paper* critic Jon Landau wrote, "I saw rock and roll's future and its name is Bruce Spring-steen. . . . He made me feel I was hearing music for the very first time."

By the mid-1970s the nation's rock fans seemed to agree with Landau. Springsteen's third album, *Born to Run* (1975) sold more than 1 million copies in just 6 weeks and dominated the top spot on the album charts. His next record, *Darkness on the Edge of Town* (1978), met with equal success. Springsteen—by now America's premier rock idol—entered the 1980s with another hit album, *The River*, and continued to compose, perform, and record with the driving energy that had propelled him from the obscurity of his early club days into the limelight of American music. Yet Springsteen never forgot his origins and continued to write songs tinged with the desperation expressed in one of his earliest hits, "Born to Run": "By day we sweat it out in the streets of a runaway American dream / At night we ride through mansions of glory in suicide machines / Baby, this town rips bones from your back / It's a death trap, a suicide rap / We gotta get out while we're young / 'Cause tramps like us, baby we were born to run."

# AN AMERICAN
# SUCCESS STORY

Now at the age of eighty-five years as I look back with
my mind's eye to the first Hollanders as they came to
this country, most of them poor, uneducated, and
lacking in practically all of the civilities of American
social life, I see them and their children, educated,
enterprising, thrifty, and prosperous, equal in every
way in social as well as in business life to any class of
people in this broad land.

This reflection by Arend Jan Brusse, immigrant
to America in 1846, sums up the success of the
Dutch Americans, an ethnic group that quickly
achieved its goals of religious freedom and economic
security in the United States. Much of the Dutch ac-
complishment can be credited to perseverance, learned
first in their homeland and then practiced in the New
World.

In the Netherlands the Dutch waged a long and hard
battle against the sea itself: The continual flooding of
their land led them to ease their lot with the ingenious
placement of dams and dikes. They were just as inven-
tive as American pioneers. Dutch prairie farmers used
pumpkins for chairs and built benches into the mud
walls of their sod houses. At Christmastime they created
a makeshift holiday tree and decorated it with twisted
tissue paper, popcorn streamers, and colored balls.

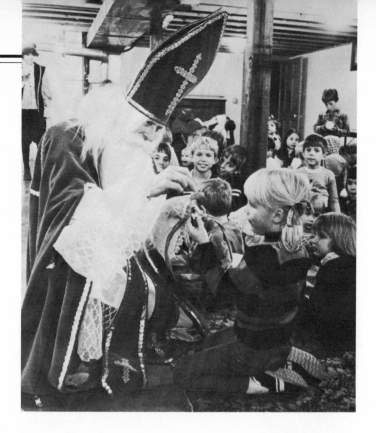

Sinterklaas, *the Dutch Santa Claus, distributes Christmas goodies in Pella, Iowa.*

Dutch Americans centered their lives around such family and community events.

In her book *Stubborn for Liberty* the historian Alice P. Kenney argues that the Dutch frequently found themselves at odds with American individualism. But in other ways the Dutch fit right into American society. Whereas other ethnic groups fought for respect, employment, or prestige in the United States, the Dutch enjoyed a privileged status from their earliest days in colonial America. In fact, the Protestant Dutch bore so many similarities to the Protestant English that they never had to shun their traditional values to gain acceptance in the colonies. Like their British counterparts, early Dutch settlers valued success in business, hard work, and plain living.

Yet the Dutch could not claim complete exemption from the stereotypes that plagued other ethnic groups. They were sometimes perceived by other Americans as greedy, miserly, and uncultured. Alexander Hamilton, a prominent patriot and the son-in-law of Dutch American Philip Schuyler, during the American Revolution, thought the Dutch were "at best rustic and unpolished" with "little desire . . . for conversation and society, their whole thoughts turned upon profit and gain." J. Hector St. Jean de Crevecoeur, an 18th-century American farmer, wrote letters in which he described the Dutch:

> [Y]ou will find his house and farm to be the neatest in all the country; and you will judge by his waggon [sic] and fat horses that he thinks more of this world than of . . . the next. He is sober and laborious; therefore he is all he ought to be as to the affairs of this life. As for those of the next, he must trust to the great Creator.

Although they were never very numerous, the Dutch Americans exerted an unexpected influence in the New World. In the field of politics Dutch Americans Philip Schuyler, Martin Van Buren, Theodore Roosevelt, and Franklin Delano Roosevelt ranked among the most important public figures of their day. Other Dutch Americans of note include the filmmaker Cecil B. DeMille, the poet Mark Van Doren and his brother, writer Carl Van Doren, the educator Clarence Dykstra, the artist Willem de Kooning, the inventor Lee De Forest, and the baseball player Len Dykstra. One of the most popular American figures—Santa Claus—also has a Dutch origin. The name comes from the Dutch word for Saint Nicholas, "Sinterklaas," and dates back to the New Netherland epoch in American history.

Over the last 300 years the Dutch seem to have successfully adapted to American life. The United States benefited from their energies here in this country and from the traditions that they brought with them from Holland. The Dutch profited from the exchange, too. They left an overcrowded country at some of its lowest points in history to come to a land that offered greater opportunity at the time. More recently, the Dutch found refuge from the hardships of war-torn Europe. For decades since then the Dutch have not needed to emigrate, but if they ever do they know that there are Americans who will welcome them. ⪧

*Karen Hammonds, an American of Dutch ancestry, poses in traditional garb on the front steps of her suburban Connecticut home in about 1969.*

# FURTHER READING

Bailey, Anthony. *The Horizon Concise History of the Low Countries.* New York: American Heritage, 1972.

Crevecoeur, J. Hector St. Jean de. *Letters from an American Farmer and Sketches of Eighteenth-Century America.* New York: Penguin, 1981.

De Jong, Gerald. *The Dutch in America, 1609–1974.* Boston: Twayne, 1975.

Irving, Washington. *History, Tales, and Sketches.* New York: Library of America, 1983.

Jameson, J. Franklin, ed. *Narratives of New Netherland, 1609–1664.* New York: Scribners, 1909.

Kenney, Alice P. *Stubborn for Liberty: The Dutch in New York.* Syracuse, NY: Syracuse University Press, 1975.

Lucas, Henry S. *Dutch Immigrant Memoirs and Related Writings.* 2 vols. Assen, Netherlands: Van Gorcum, 1955.

Miller, Nathan. *The Roosevelt Chronicles: The Story of a Great American Family.* Garden City, NY: Doubleday, 1979.

# INDEX

# PICTURE CREDITS

VICTORIA OLSON is a graduate of Barnard College and a lifetime resident of New York City. A descendant of Melchior Keator, an employee of the Dutch West India Company in New Netherland, she first became interested in the Dutch through genealogical research. She is currently studying English literature at Stanford University.

DANIEL PATRICK MOYNIHAN is the senior United States senator from New York. He is also the only person in American history to serve in the cabinets or subcabinets of four successive presidents—Kennedy, Johnson, Nixon, and Ford. Formerly a professor of government at Harvard University, he has written and edited many books, including *Beyond the Melting Pot, Ethnicity: Theory and Experience* (both with Nathan Glazer), *Loyalties,* and *Family and Nation.*

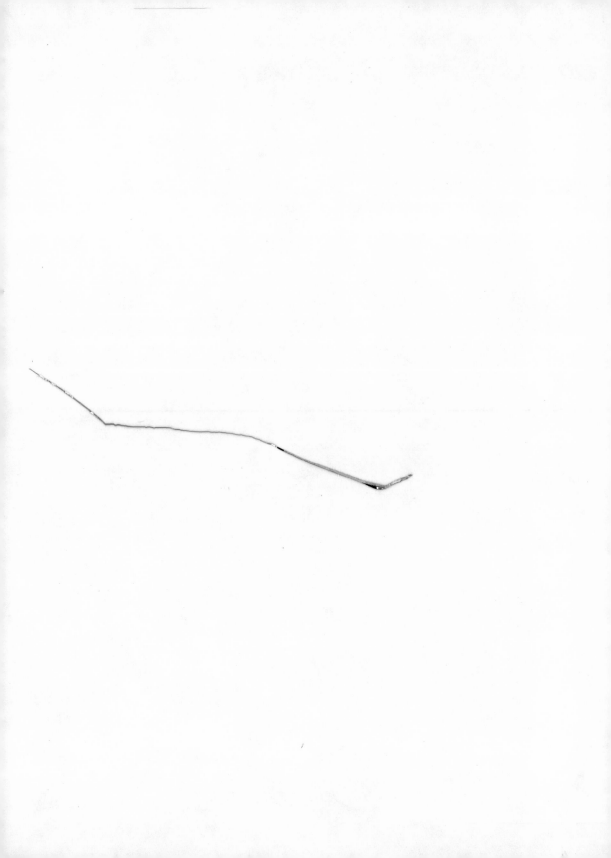